Gemini Joe

Janet Sierzant

Gemini Joe

Copyright ©2009 by Janet Sierzant

Published by La Maison Publishing, Inc.
www.lamaisonpub.com

Library of Congress Control Number: 2009909341

ISBN: 978-0-615-29041-6

Gemini Joe is based on a true story. Some names have been changed to protect the identities of select individuals.

Editing by Susan Cochran
www.writtencopy.com

Bookcover and layout design by Lisa M. Russell
www.russellink.org

Purchase more copies at *www.lamaisonpub.com*

Acknowledgements

I would like to thank Kennesaw State University and the English Department. The Writing Lab staff worked with my first drafts and encouraged me to continue writing and polishing my work. I am grateful to the Georgia Writers Association for the resourceful workshops, knowledgeable speakers, and other Georgia Writers who took time from their writing to read and comment on my book. To my editor, Sue Cochran, and my graphic designer, Lisa M. Russell, who guided me through the process of publication.

Table of Contents

Prologue xi
Chapter One. 15
Chapter Two 29
Chapter Three 39
Chapter Four 48
Chapter Five. 58
Chapter Six. 67
Chapter Seven 77
Chapter Eight. 91
Chapter Nine 99
Chapter Ten 111
Chapter Eleven 124
Chapter Twelve 131
Chapter Thirteen 137
Chapter Fourteen 150
Chapter Fifteen 162
Chapter Sixteen 170
Chapter Seventeen 186
Chapter Eighteen. 198
Epilogue 216
Photographs. 222

This is a story of a man, a man that preferred to live his life playing a victim, even though he had the potential to do great things. If he was just any man, I'd be able to ignore the havoc he inflicted on those around him, but this man is my father. I should feel love, but I find myself indifferent.

– Janet Sierzant

Poems

For a Moment	xii
Be Yourself	14
To Be or Not to Be	28
A True Friend	38
Memories	47
Games of Play	57
A Silent Tear	66
The Falcon	76
The Fear of Death	90
Absence	98
One and Only	104
Return to the Woods	110
A Gift	123
Time	130
The Sounds of a Waterfall	136
Thoughts of Peace	149
Peaches and Cream	152
Each Day of Our Lives	161
Butterfly	169
Drinking Man's Lament	170
Cold and Lonely Night	181
Who is to Blame	185
Lost Treasures	187
A Special Friend	189
Regrets and Tears	190
Share a Log	195
Forgotten Love	197
My Shadow is Cast	200
Scooter's Den	204
Lonely Heart	208
Light of Life	215

Prologue

Joseph Fuccino sits alone in his trailer. His only companion is the television. Every morning he gropes along the wall, inching the way from his bed to his urine-stained reclining chair, fearing he might fall. He feebly reaches for the hose of his oxygen tank and sucks the air in slow, deliberate spurts. Sixty years of smoking have caught up with him and he knows he will die from complications of emphysema, the same disease that killed his father. At first glance, one might feel sympathy for this man. They would have no way of knowing how he affected his family.

* * * * * *

The earliest memory Anna had of her father is from a family wedding when she was four years old. She could still see her mother smiling and dancing, happy to be surrounded by the music and people. Anna's father sat at a table, glaring as her lovely frame glided across the dance floor. He drank one scotch on the rocks after another until jealousy took hold of him and rage cut the evening short. Driving home in a drunken stupor, he argued with and yelled at his wife as he stomped on the gas pedal.

"You had to be the belle of the ball, flirting with all those men, didn't you?" He snarled.

Anna cowered on the floor in the back seat, praying they would not die. She felt the car tipping to one side and whispered, "Please, Daddy, don't," as he sped around the curves.

This was the beginning of what her life was to be and, as she grew older, Anna learned to distance herself from his frequent tirades. He spent most of his time at the bar, where they knew him as "Gemini Joe," a charismatic, funny man who was the life of any party. His family rarely saw the funny side of him at home. A bottle of scotch on the table was all it took to set him off, causing his children to hide at the top of the stairs, listening and waiting for the fighting to end. Finally, on the downside of his drunken spells, the yelling subsided as Joe transitioned into the "crying game." He was predictable in his tears. After all the damage he caused, he wanted to be the victim. His children forgave him with words but not with their hearts.

The marital problems between Anna's father and mother started before she was born. She was stuck in the middle of their madness, along with her two sisters and brother. Being the oldest, she was able to disappear without being noticed, leaving her younger siblings to fend for themselves. Anna felt guilty but she was in survival mode, and they all learned to adapt to the unstable environment. Years of fighting and turmoil followed until it became a natural state of family life. Anna's father alienated everyone around him and no one escaped his accusations. He remained a stranger for most of her life, and she only saw brief moments of his true character when he was not drunk or angry. She wanted to love him but found him difficult to please. She wanted to please him but knew it was impossible. After years of silence, she received a letter along with a poem that changed her life. It said:

> *"The name of this poem is 'For a Moment,' because at the time I wrote it, it seemed as though everything important and good, the things that made me feel good, only seemed to last but a moment! Anna, I love you and think of you always. Some day we will meet again, hug again, and kiss again. Love Always, Dad."*

> *We gathered the pearls of the Ocean,*
> *For a moment,*
> *We counted the Stars in the Sky,*
> *For a Moment,*
> *We showed our Emotions,*
> *And then, in a moment, we said*
> *Good bye!*

Impressed by his words and surprised that she did not know this side of her father, she asked him to send more of the writings that expressed his feelings about life. Most of it was dark, depressed and moody while some of it was childlike and simple, but it allowed Anna to empathize with the feelings he experienced during those turbulent times. Just beneath his anger, an emotional neediness sucked up energy like a sponge. Anna began to wonder about his childhood, which she knew little about. His past molded him into the person he became and Anna's curiosity grew. He was never her daddy but he was her father, and she wanted to know what happened to him in his life to make him bitter and cynical. Anna was determined to retrieve what was rightfully hers. He never spoke about his childhood or his family, and no one ever asked until now.

Be Yourself

I'm not the man I used to be
And think about it much
I'd like to see those days again
When it use to be as such

I stood as tall as an old oak tree
Not being anyone but me
Time and wisdom took its toll
Wearing down my very soul

Words can sometimes cause us hurt
When searching for the truth
Telling someone how to grow
    Destroys their fragile root

Stand by your convictions
With a mellow tone
Face up to contradictions
Without a frown or groan

— Gemini Joe

Chapter One
New York, 1929

"Where is he?" Florence screamed as the labor pains became more intense.

As usual, her husband was out drinking, gambling and chasing women. She did not intend to have another baby after eight years, but her obsession to keep him home in his own bed put her at risk. At first she thought having another baby was a blessing and believed it would bring the family closer together, but the last three months of the pregnancy kept only her in their bed.

"How can he leave me alone to have his bastard by myself?" she yelled in a fit of pain. No one was home except her ten-year-old daughter. There was no time to go to the hospital. Florence would have to give birth at home. Her daughter Dolly's young eyes were as big as saucers, but she did her best to follow her mother's instructions, bringing clean sheets and hot water to her bedside. The labor was hard and Florence cursed her unborn baby with every painful push. After a scream that made Dolly cover her ears, the baby appeared.

"Go in the kitchen and get the knife with the white handle," Florence told her daughter.

Dolly stood frozen, staring down at her mother and the pool of blood surrounding the baby.

"Go now!" Her mother yelled.

When the young girl returned with the knife, she closed her eyes tightly, thinking that her mother was going to kill her new baby brother. Finally, she opened them to see the baby was still alive, swaddled in one of the sheets and lying on her mother's chest.

"He's so cute," she squealed as she gently reached for the baby. "Can I hold him?" There was no way for Dolly to know that the novelty would wear off and, in time, she would grow to resent caring for her brother.

The baby boy had already made his entrance into the world by the time his father, Joseph, stumbled through the front door well after midnight. With liquor on his breath, he peered down at his fourth child.

"Joseph the second," he slurred, and then passed out on the couch.

* * * * * *

In the summer of 1903, twenty-year-old Domenico Fuccino stood on the deck of the Manuel Calvo along with his fellow passengers from Naples. Before he set foot on the boat that would carry him across the Atlantic Ocean, he struggled with the fear of rumors he heard around the village. Stories about America, the "Land of the Free," contradicted claims that being an Italian was the exception. Few made it past their Irish predecessors to make a living, but laborers were needed to build the sewer system. Some Italians decided to take their chances in the new world, using their skills with brick, stone and cement.

"You do not know masonry," Domenico's father frowned. "How will you make money?"

"Americans wear clothes, don't they?" He argued with his father. "I could sew for a big company in New York." Domenico did not know the difference between mortar and cement, but he was good with a needle and thread.

"You'll be back," his father promised.

Domenico pushed his father's words out of his mind and stared out at the ocean. Salty mist sprayed his face and he tightened his coat across his chest. Even when he was wet and shivering, he stayed on deck, refusing to go below to the crowded steerage except to catch a few hours of sleep.

For two weeks clouds snuffed out the sun as storms attacked the ship, one after another. The constant chatter of voices blended into the sounds of the sea until he no longer heard them. It was the silence that rang in his ears as the passengers gazed out to sea. The sun peeked out, and the Statue of Liberty could be seen in the distance. Everyone began to cheer, "God Bless America!"

It was July 4th.. The sun went down as the ship drew closer to the New York harbor, and the sky darkened. Waves slapped against the boat, allowing the cold ocean to jump onto the boat. The passengers were retreating below deck when a young boy yelled, "Look!" and pointed to the sky. Their eyes followed his finger to the colorful rockets exploding in the skyline. Everyone pushed and shoved their way back up to the deck. With each shower of sparks, the great lady holding her torch illuminated in a beacon of hope.

Their journey was coming to an end. Each person turned inward to his or her own dreams and anticipations for a new life. But before entering their new home, each passenger would have to pass a medical examination on Ellis Island. Domenico's uncle referred to it as "Isola della Lacrime," the Island of Tears, because many people were sent back to their country of origin.

Single-file they marched through the brick building on Ellis Island, hoping some underlying illness did not betray them and put them on the waiting ship back to Italy. Domenico inched his way up the line, nervously turning the hat in his hands. It was a special hat. He made it for the journey to America and planned to use it as a prototype when he opened his haberdashery. He had a skill and a dream. He also had a cousin waiting for him in Manhattan, willing to take him in until he could get on his feet.

Domenico was asked many questions about his origins and why he wanted to come to America. He tried to hide his runny nose.

"How long have you had that cold, son?"

"It's almost gone," Domenico promised.

"Make yourself comfortable, young man; you'll be staying with us for a few days."

Domenico sighed. His cousin was waiting on the other side. He felt confused and alone until, through the thunderous noise and chatter, he heard someone speaking Italian. Heading toward the source of communication, he met two Sicilian brothers from a small fishing village in Palermo. The three men followed the crowd into a huge dining room. They wrinkled their noses at the strange smells coming from the gigantic pots. Domenico bite into a hot dog then spat it back into his dish. He drank the milk, but wished that he had more.

Every day they walked to the gate leading to the ferries that crossed the harbor. As soon his cold went away, he was allowed to leave. When he stepped onto the ferry, he felt a rush of freedom. As they neared the dock, faces of the waiting people came into focus and he could hear them yelling greetings to their relatives.

Gemini Joe

He ran up and down the ship trying to find an opening among the other passengers. Anxiously, he looked for his cousin as the crew secured the ship to the dock. When he saw the multitudes of people waiting on shore, Domenico began to panic.

"How am I going to find Thomas in this mass of humanity?" His eyes searched the crowd as he walked down the plank. He stood among the people, searching, as they hugged and greeted each other. The crowd thinned and Domenico was alone. He looked down at the ticket that had brought him to this place. A summer breeze blew the paper trash, dancing in the wind as it swirled around in a circle and then blew off into the distance. He breathed the July air deeply and walked toward two cops standing at the corner of a building to ask for help. But the smile on their faces deceived him.

One was twirling his baton as if he was itching to use it. They both stared down the crowd. "Stupid Wops," one said, loud enough for him to hear.

"Yeah, just what we need around here," replied his partner, "more Guineas."

Domenico stopped before they realized he was coming toward them. This was not the welcome that he had expected. Suddenly, someone came up from behind and grabbed him by the shoulders, swinging him around until they were face to face.

"Tommy!" he yelled with joy before cursing his cousin for scaring him half to death. "What's with them?" he asked, as they collected his belongings and walked out of the boatyard.

"Who, those Irish Micks in uniform?" Tommy smirked. "Don't worry about them. Just make sure you get off the streets by 10 p.m. That's when they go hunting, and you don't want to face the billy clubs in some dark alley. Uncle Bruno had his knees bashed one night when he was returning from his job washing dishes. They threatened to crack his head open if they ever caught him out at night."

Domenico worried that the rumors were true, but he was not alone. Italian people banded together, joining clubs and charters where they united to protect each other from the prejudices of the Irish.

Little Italy was formed with a mix of small merchants and laborers. Some sold fruits and vegetables from a cart on the corner while others opened bakeries or taverns where the men socialized in their native language. They gathered to discuss news of Italy and promote Italian culture.

Domenico met Antoinette at the Catholic Church they attended, and asked her out on a date. Born in New York, she was already an American citizen.

"I'll help you study for the exam," she offered. "You'll have your papers in no time."

It was a double celebration when he was awarded citizenship. In his happiness, he proposed to Antoinette. After the wedding, the babies began to arrive. One son after another was born. He worked harder to save his money.

Domenico worked in a textile factory, and mended clothing at night for extra money. It took him seven years before he saved enough to open his own hat store on Mott Street. He stood back and admired the sign outside his new shop, then laughed to himself as he recalled his father's warning. Customers, all Italian, came to buy a hat.

One day, he looked up from his workbench to see a strange man with red curly hair.

"Can I help you?"

"Yes, I would like to order me a hat," the Irishman said in a thick brogue.

"Of course," Domenico said as he grabbed his measuring tape. "I just need to make some calculations." He wrapped the tape around the man's head and gasped.

"Is something wrong?" Patrick asked.

"No, no!" he said. This is a big head, he thought to himself.

"It will be ready next week," he promised.

When the man returned, Domenico lifted the hat from its box and placed it on his customer's head.

"It's perfect!" the man said.

The cash register clanged when the draw opened, and Domenico smiled.

The next day, the Irishman was back.

"Signore, this hat you made for me, it's too big. Can you adjust it?"

Domenico felt obliged to fit the hat properly, but he was annoyed. "You said the hat was good when you picked it up," he said, trying not to show his annoyance.

"I thought it was good, but I was wrong."

The milliner went to work, re-measuring the man's head.

"It will take some work, but I can make it smaller," he told the man.

"Thank you," the Irishman said and walked toward the door. "I will come back tomorrow."

Domenico worked late into the night, taking out the stitches and making the hat smaller. The next day, the Irishman returned.

"Thank you. It's perfect."

Two days later, the Irishman was standing in front of him, once more.

"What now?" Domenico snapped.

"Well, you did a good job. It is smaller, but something is not right."

Domenico's blood began to boil, but he kept his composure as he examined the hat. "It looks fine to me."

"Perhaps you could loosen the band a little," the Irishman pleaded.

"All right, come back tomorrow."

When the Irishman returned the next day, Domenico was sure the hat would fit. He placed it on his head.

"How's that?" He asked as he held up a mirror.

The Irishman stood looking at himself and a smile crawled across his lips.

"I guess I shouldn't have gotten that haircut this morning," he said. "Now the hat is too big again."

Domenico's face turned crimson and his eyes protruded from his head. He could not contain himself a minute longer. "Here, let me fix it," he said, as he yanked the hat down over the Irishman's eyes. He stood with his head poking through the hat as it lay around his neck. Domenico grabbed the Irishman by the back of his shirt and pushed him through the front door, Italian curses pouring from his lips. "Don't ever come back to my store again," he yelled as the Irishman scurried down the street.

A few days later, the front bell jingled, and a big burly man in a blue uniform stepped into his shop.

"Are you Domenico Fuccino," he barked.

"Yes, that's me," Domenico nervously replied.

"I had a complaint about you," the Irish cop snarled.

That Irishman! Domenico thought.

"What did I do?"

"I heard that you assaulted one of your customers."

His eyes scanned the merchandise and he began trying one hat after another, studying his reflection in the mirror.

"I may decide to take you down to the station," he threatened.

"I don't want trouble," Domenico said, biting his tongue as the cop defiled his wares.

"This one was made for me," he announced, his blue eyes gleaming.

"Yes," Domenico slowly replied. "It fits you well. Please take it as a gift from me."

"Make sure I don't have any more trouble from you," the policeman said as he left with the hat.

Domenico spit on the ground after he was gone. He did not realize that his young son, Joseph, was watching from the backroom. Joseph felt embarrassed by his father's weakness. He vowed never to let someone to treat him like that. After all, this was America; land of the free and home of the brave.

* * * * * *

Joseph was born with his father's hot-tempered nature and stubborn streak, and he made no effort to control it. Even as a youngster, he was heard throughout the neighborhood as his voice carried far beyond the open windows of the brick building where he lived. "I want a penny! I want a penny! I want a penny!" he repeated, until his mother gave in.

Joseph was the eldest of four brothers: Tom, Charlie, Pat and himself. Their mother, Antoinette, did not have a chance against all those boys although she tried her best to harness their aggression. The slightest thing would set them off and they would roll around the floor, punching and hitting each other until someone got hurt. Antoinette tried to break them up but was usually rewarded with scars. The fights did not last long, though, and soon they packed up their aggression and took it outside. But no matter what problems there were within the family, they stayed in the family. On the street, they had each other's back.

They grew up between Mulberry and Mott Street, where they learned the meaning of Italian unity and its uses in warding off the injustices of the world. Joseph watched his father struggle to earn a living and humble himself to people around him in order to avoid the Mob. A growing disdain developed in his heart and he saw his father as a weak man who refused to take advantage of the benefits of his Italian heritage. At nineteen years old, Joseph decided he wanted more out of life than he was willing to put in. He drank too much, smoked too much and gambled, dragging his three younger brothers along with him.

Tom, Charlie and Pat were no match for Joseph, who was clearly was the boss of the brothers. Together they walked down Mulberry Street, daring anyone to mess with them. They had to be tough. Life was not easy. The city streets were unforgiving and fights broke out over the smallest infractions. The four Fuccino brothers had an attitude and a reputation, and they enjoyed the sport. If someone picked a fight with one, they would soon face the wrath of all. Whether they were betting on the horses or hanging out at the beach or church dances, girls were attracted to the danger.

Joseph looked outside of his home for validity, admiring the respect that some Italian people demanded. He turned his back on the work ethic his parents tried to drum into him and learned how to survive by making easy money with the Mob, working as a bookie and taking bets instead of working at a laborious job.

Determination and toughness made Joseph a man to be respected by the families in charge, but his loyalty lay with the Giovanni family, who recruited him to run the rackets. Joseph proudly represented their ruthlessness. His brothers were aware of the family's history and the price they would pay for getting involved. They decided not to be a part of it, which devastated their older brother.

"Go work in the factories," he yelled. "Don't come crying to me for money."

Money did flow, and Joseph drove fancy cars and dressed in the finest clothes. He was generous to his family in spite of his threats. His mother begrudgingly accepted his money to survive, not wanting to know the details of how it was earned. Unemployment was high and the profits from the haberdashery were not enough to put food on the table. The Depression had its grip on New York City. Domenico knew he was not the main breadwinner in his family. He accepted his son's money but spit on the ground at the mention of his name.

* * * * * *

Joseph married a woman just like his mother. She also turned a blind eye to his methods of bringing money into their home. Florence put up with a great deal from her husband. Florence's mother, Carmella, wished her son-in-law would fall off the edge of the earth whenever she noticed a new bruise on her daughter, but she knew he would outlive everyone. If her husband was alive, he would have forbidden his daughter from marrying a man like Joseph Fuccino, but Carmella did not have the power to persuade her young daughter.

Carmella arrived in America in 1911 with her husband, Franc, six-year-old Florence and her other four children on The Sant' Anna. It was a hard journey, but they looked forward to a new beginning. Franc was ready to work hard for his family. His brother's family welcomed him and his family into their home until he could save for a place of his own. After pounding the concrete for months and doing odd jobs for food money, he secured a job as a steel worker. Building bridges and tall buildings paid very well, but it was hard work. Franc could have taken the easy way out as a carrier for a neighborhood bookie, but he wanted to make an honest living.

Franc Mazio sat on his perch at the top of what would be the Brooklyn Bridge, high above New York. Steel beams floated through the sky, held only by a chain. "Steady, steady," the foreman yelled through his megaphone to the crane operator as he swung his cargo into place. Creaking chains seemed to moan under the weight of the steel and pierced the ears of the immigrant workers who labored all day for the $2.25 in Italian guineas. A sense of confusion took over as the constant sound of drills and hammers met steel, shooting a fury of sparks into the hot, humid air. Franc had to be careful not to look at the flare from the welders, which had a temporary blinding effect. The summer was sweltering and the steel absorbed the heat of the sun. As the sweat streamed down his dirty face, Franc thought the fires of Hell couldn't be hotter!

But when winter came, Franc wished for the molten smell of hot steel as he clutched his thin coat close to his chest. The icy wind cut into his skin like a knife. It whipped around the bridge and buildings high above the city, taking with it anything that was not secure. He was glad when the foreman gave him the sign to break for lunch. Franc fought the wind as he folded back the wrapping of the sandwich Carmella packed for him.

"Daddy, I put a surprise in your lunch," Florence, whispered as she kissed him goodbye. Franc smiled as he reached into his lunch bag. He pulled out an apple, wrapped in pink paper with hearts. "I love you," it said in crayon and glitter. He smiled as the cold, long bars of steel moved past his head. He had wanted to be a policeman but there was a height requirement of 5'7" and most Italian men fell short. He set that dream aside to support his family.

The sound of rusted steel creaked and moaned. "Steady, steady," the foreman repeated as the beam wobbled. Franc looked up from his lunch and watched as the slow-moving steel came his way. The force of contact was quick and solid as the beam hit Franc in the head, the apple tumbling from his hand toward the sea. Steel on steel crushed bones and severed the limbs of those who were not alert. Carmella, left alone to raise her two sons and three daughters in the house Franc provided for his family, never remarried.

The Depression didn't affect the Mazios like it did other families because Franc made sure they would be taken care of in the event of his death. He took out an insurance policy on his life, knowing the risks of his occupation. It was a quiet life and they were a quiet people, doing their best to carve out a place in their new land.

Fair-skinned with auburn hair that glowed like fire when hit by the sun, Florence had the classic look of a Roman beauty. Chiseled features highlighted her high cheekbones and Italian nose, but people rarely noticed her nose because her hazel eyes caught their attention instead. Her eyes changed color with her clothing, sometimes blue, sometimes green, sometimes gold.

Born in 1905 and named after the town of her birth in Italy, she grew up with all the grace of her Italian culture, learning to cook and sing opera. At fifteen years old, Florence loved the beach. Everyday she walked to the boardwalk with her two sisters, Jenny and Mary, where she first met Joseph Fuccino. Joseph went to the boardwalk with his brothers to check out the girls on those long summer days. He wasn't as interested in her as she was in him, but Florence pursued him and did everything she could to get his attention.

"Slow down," Jenny said as her sister moved at a rapid pace down the street, her eyes looking straight ahead toward her destination.

"Wait for us," Mary called after her. But Florence refused.

She had to get to the boardwalk. Joseph might be there and she didn't want him to catch the eye of another girl. By the end of the summer, her flirting paid off and she became his steady girl. Joseph was strong in body and soul. He filled the hole that her father's death created, protecting Florence and making her feel as if she was his special possession.

"I don't want you coming to the beach without me," he insisted. "I don't like the way guys look at you."

"Don't be silly," Florence replied. "I've been coming here for years with my sisters. Nothing is going to..."

The look in Joseph's eyes warned her to shut up. "All right," she agreed. "I don't want you to worry."

Florence loved being with Joseph. He kissed her tenderly under the boardwalk, making her forget the cruel words he occasionally spit at her. She could never stay mad at him for long and looked forward to their time together at their special place in the sand.

By the end of the summer, Florence sensed that Joseph was holding back his emotions. She caught him eyeing other girls when he thought she wasn't looking, which made her jealous but she pretended she didn't see. She was afraid that fighting about it would only give him a reason to break up with her. Instead, she went out of her way to please him, but she never gained his respect. Like a bad habit, Joseph kept her around but his desire for other women could not be tamed. She knew he was unfaithful.

Florence's persistence paid off and within a year, Joseph bent under her pressure to get married.

"I don't like him. He is never going to make you happy," her mother warned.

"He'll change once we are married," Florence assured her.

"But you are only fifteen. You're too young to get married."

"I love him and I don't want to lose him! I'll die if I can't marry him now."

Against her mother's wishes, she dropped out of school to marry Joseph.

They had a small, elegant wedding, but whispers hummed among the guests.

"He's five years older than her. He's robbing the cradle," one aunt whispered to another.

"He'll never settle down," a cousin whispered to a friend.

In spite of the rumors, everyone smiled and wished them good luck. Florence got what she wanted, and Joseph got a maid and child-bearer for his children. He agreed to leave Little Italy for Coney Island so his wife could be close to her family, and they moved into a small apartment down the street from Florence's mother. Together they produced four children. Antoinette, named after her father's mother, was the oldest, but everyone called her Dolly because she was the only girl in a family of boys. Then the twins arrived, Domenico and Franc, named after each grandfather. Joey was the baby of the family, with a ten-year difference between him and his sister. Joey was born on the tenth day of June, 1929; the year the Great Depression began. He had big brown eyes and a head full of brown curls. He quickly won the hearts of his family, who treated him like a toy or a pet, playing with him until they tired.

Born with a heart murmur and chronic bronchitis, Joey had to be watched at all times. Breathing problems made him the center of attention and every time he coughed or could not catch his breath, his parents piled the whole family in the car and drove to a small creek in Coney Island. On the way, Joey was allowed to hang his head out the car window to get fresh air. As they drew closer, the smell of rotten eggs filled the car. The sulfur fumes from the creek helped him breathe, and soon little Joey felt better.

Joey was a finicky eater and his mother tried everything to camouflage vegetables by hiding them in the mashed potatoes and distracting him with stories as he ate.

She said, "Okay, Joey, take a bite, and I will tell you the story of Jack and the Bean Stalk."

Joey was very interested and put the fork in his mouth, holding the food on his tongue without swallowing.

His mother stopped the story mid-sentence and said, "Swallow, or I can't finish the story."

Once he did, she continued. Jack and the Bean Stalk, Little Red Riding Hood, Snow White. She narrated so well that Joey soon forgot he was eating. Later in life, he credited his mother for any storytelling talent he may have inherited. Joey always felt safe when he was with his mother. She was the guiding force in his life as he struggled to avoid the harshness of his father and brothers.

* * * * * *

Joseph had made money doing small jobs for the Mob on Mulberry Street, but now that he lived in Coney Island, he had less work.

"I don't want you making that kind of money," Florence pleaded. "I'll get a job until you find real work." But making a decent living was difficult. Florence earned money sewing Pea coats for the navy at a local mercantile factory. Rows of tables with sewing machines filled the warehouse. The hum never ceased as the fabric ran under the needle quickly bobbing up and down, powered by delicate feet.

Florence's hands had a permanent blue tint from handling the dye of the material. Even when she scrubbed them, she couldn't erase the stains. The blue pigment entered into the pores of her skin and, like a mechanic with black grease under his fingernails, it was accepted as part of the job.

Because it was piecework, Florence sometimes had to work around the clock. Occasionally she took Joey with her. Joey was surprised to find out that his mother was not the only lady with blue hands. He loved the attention from the factory women who cooed at everything he did or said.

"What a good boy," they said as he collected all the straight pins that fell under the tables.

To Be or Not To Be

God has given to man
All that abounds on the earth
As a gift and a burden
From the day of one's birth

Making man responsible
For all his needs and pleasures
To care for all its keepings
And protect them like his treasures

To look at life as he looks in a mirror
All that he projects, good or evil,
Reward is greater than he gives
As a mirror returns a larger image

— Gemini Joe

Chapter Two

Joseph and his family lived in a Railroad Flat Apartment on Coney Island. At times there was much joy in the four-room, cold-water flat on Coney Island, where they huddled in the kitchen to keep warm by the stove. The bathroom was in the hallway because they shared it with three other families in the building. But the kitchen was the most important room, not only for the warmth but also for the food that was prepared for hungry mouths. Everyone's faces would light up when Florence came through the door with grocery bags and a bag of quarters for the electric meter, which had to be fed to keep the lights on. One quarter provided about two hours of electricity, and the service man at Con-Ed came every month to collect the fees.

Florence would sometimes carry a loaf or two of Italian bread, which she bought for a penny a loaf when the bakery wagons unloaded stale bread. The stale loaves did not last long. As soon as people saw the wagon out front, they flooded into the bakery, pushing and shoving to get their share. Florence wrapped the stale bread in damp dishtowels overnight. Like magic, by morning the bread was soft and moist. She cut it long ways and spread olive oil across the middle, sprinkling garlic, parsley, and oregano on the slices before popping it in the stove heated by burning paper, wood and coal. It was so good a king's feast couldn't have tasted better.

She was always in the kitchen and the rest of the family stayed close by. The kids sat around the table, forks in hand, waiting for dinner while Dad sneaked up behind her, turned and winked at his children, then nuzzled against her neck, kissing her and biting her ear. "Stop that," she'd say, as she hit him with a stick of spaghetti. "Not in front of the children." Joey could not contain his laughter and loved to watch his parents banter back and forth. At these times, it was easier to forgive his father for the tears Joey watched his mother shed. His father's cruelty seemed to disappear like a distant nightmare, and Joey thought maybe he did love his mother after all.

Joey thought his mom was the loveliest person in his life. Everyone loved Florence's generous heart and the happiness she wore on her face every day. She sang along with the radio during the hour-long Italian program every Saturday as she cleaned the apartment. The walls of the apartment were not very thick so, after each song, the neighbors yelled, "Encore, encore, Señora." She was a beautiful singer.

Across the street from their apartment building was the Renkins Milk Company, which had a large stable for the horses and wagons they used to deliver milk every day. Joey loved horses and spent hours in the big stable petting them. In the back of the alleyway was a blacksmith named Mike. He was a big burly Italian who smoked guinea cigars that smelled like old feet. Every day he took a horse from the milk stable across the street to his shop. Little Joey, only five years old, was very interested and hung around the blacksmith shop. Mike said, "Hey, little feller," when he noticed Joey watching him heat up the horseshoes. He picked up the horse's foot to determine the size of shoe needed and then began to mold it on his anvil. The shop was smoky and loud, but Joey loved the sound of the clinking metal as the blacksmith wielded his hammer. He noticed the steady beat as Mike struck the horseshoe in a certain way. Dot dota-dot-dot, dot-dot. Of course, everyone used that beat to knock on doors, but by banging first on the anvil and then striking the horseshoe, maybe he had a better aim at it; at least, this is what Joey decided and thought himself very clever.

Joey stood on the fence bar looking deep into a brown mare's eyes while Mike hammered on her back hoof. A feeling of mutual love between the horse and Joey filled the air, and the horse twitched and shuffled as if she wanted to go to him. All of a sudden, the horse and Joey were startled out of their connecting gaze. "Stand still, stupid, or I'll make glue out of you!" the old man yelled as he began punching the horse in her head. "Stay still!" The old man punched the horse once more for emphasis.

Joey was stunned. "Don't hit her!" he cried.

He could see Mike's yellow teeth clenching his cigar as he laughed. Joey could not bear to see cruelty. He saw enough of that at home when his father had had too much to drink. This was different, though. At home, his mother had a choice. She could leave her abusive husband if she wanted to, but the horse was trapped—a victim without a voice. Joey jumped down from the fence and ran home as fast as his short, chubby legs would carry him. Tears rolled down his checks even though he tried his best to suppress them. He stood outside of his apartment until he could dry his eyes. His brothers could smell weakness a mile away and he did not want to suffer the same fate as the horse. The next day, he walked past the blacksmith. He could hear Mike hammering away at the horse's feet but decided not to go and watch.

* * * * * *

"Joseph, please, I need more time to pay back the money I owe."
"You've had plenty of time. I can't do business like this."
"Please! I'm trying to pay you back."
"You're a good man, Lou, but you have a gambling problem."
"I know! I'll stop! I promise."
"Your gambling is not my problem. You need to pay me now!" Joseph said, firmly.
"All I have is my business. You can take it. Please!" the man begged.
"What do I want with a luncheonette?" Joseph asked.
"You can keep it for your family. It's a good business and it will make you money," the man promised.

Joseph stared in disgust at the man in front of him. Just as he was about to throw him out of his apartment, he had an idea. Maybe it would be just the thing to keep his wife busy. She loved cooking and had too much time on her hands. He hoped that maybe she would stop following him whenever he went out at night. Florence was always dressed and ready to leave the house, ripping off her apron at a moment's notice. "Dolly, watch your brother," Florence instructed her daughter as she grabbed her coat and slammed the door behind her, already in pursuit of her husband. Joseph often saw Florence in the shadows, watching as he left the bar, but he said nothing to spare her the embarrassment.

He sat the family around the table to announce their new business venture. "I was given a luncheonette," he told his family. "It has a candy store in the front and an apartment above."

Florence sat silently while the boys excitedly discussed the benefits.

"We will have all the candy we could eat!" the twins said.

Joey jumped up and down at the prospect. Joey looked up to his father. He was the strongest man he knew and had many friends who showered him with gifts.

"Does that mean we have to move?" Florence asked.

"Yes, but the apartment is bigger and the electric is included. It's going to be great, you'll see. The kids can help."

They moved into the small two-bedroom apartment above the store. Florence worked long hours, cooking tomato sauce and lasagna. Joseph was in charge of making the Italian ices. There was only one flavor: lemon. The children sat at the table with a big bucket of cut lemons and were instructed to squeeze out the fragrant juice. At first it was fun, but after a while, their fingers stung from the acidity of the fruit and they whined until their father took over.

Joey was so proud of his mom in her luncheonette uniform. She looked so beautiful. Her curly hair escaped the bun on her head and fell in front of her eyes as she cooked the sauce in big pots over the stoves. By the end of the day, tomato sauce, meatballs and spaghetti stained her nice white apron, but Joey thought she looked great. She was loved in the neighborhood and never refused a customer extra sauce or bread, even though it annoyed Joseph. "How are we going to make any money if you keep giving the food away?" Joseph complained.

Florence winked at her youngest son, who sat at a counter stool eating the graham crackers she crushed up in his milk. She was the light of the family and had a way of soothing the aggression of her sons and husband, keeping their tempers at a low boil.

While his parents worked, Joey spent a lot of time with his grandmother, Carmella. Sometimes he stayed with his grandmother for days until his mother came to get him. Carmella gave her grandson a buttered roll and dried his tears whenever he cried. Joey felt like he was a burden to his family because a small child made life harder during the Depression. He was convinced that if he were a good boy, his parents would not send him away. He learned to please the adults around him, to make them laugh, and he tried always to be cute.

Old age was creeping up on Nana and some days arthritis swelled her joints, making it hard for her to walk. On the rare occasions when she was feeling well, she took Joey to the boardwalk at Coney Island. They rode the trolley that passed by his grandmother's house. Carmella lied about Joey's age to get him on free, but the conductor was wise to her tricks and tried to argue. "My grandson is under five," she claimed.

"This boy is at least six years old," the trolley conductor said.

"Pay, Nana, please pay," Joey pleaded.

Nevertheless, she never backed down to save the nickel fare. They walked up and down the boardwalk, listening to the music and watching the people. Walking on the boardwalk, Joey couldn't keep his eyes off the parachute tower that loomed above his head. People were dropping out of the air and he was sure they were going to splatter on the ground. Of course, the ropes and the parachutes stopped them from plunging to the earth. But he was a child and the sheer terror of falling made him close his eyes.

Sometimes Nana let him ride on the merry-go-round. If you could catch the gold ring as you went around, you won a free ride, but it was hard for Joey so he didn't try. He preferred the middle horse that went up and down. It always had to be the black horse with the white mane. He named it Blackie.

As they walked along the boardwalk, Joey noticed his grandmother drinking from a small, silver flask. "Can I have some, Nana?" he asked.

"No, baby, this is my medicine," she replied, as she took a swig and put it back in her purse.

Most of the time she spoke to him in Italian, and he picked it up pretty well, until his father heard him. "We are in America," he yelled. "Speak English."

Joey's father reacted to the discrimination toward Italian people in New York and found it hard to be proud of his background. Joseph firmly believed that assimilation was the answer, which meant losing the language and culture of the old country. When Joey grew up, he resented his father's narrow-minded views of what being American meant. Joey spent the rest of his life trying to validate his ethnicity.

* * * * * *

Gemini Joe

Joey loved the holidays, mostly because of his mother, who was always in the kitchen cooking the holiday feast. Food was the centerpiece of their family celebrations. Joey loved to watch her from his high stool, which she set in the kitchen so he could see everything but also so she could keep an eye on him. Every Easter she baked pies for the neighbors who came to wish a happy holiday. Grain pies, salami pies, ricotta pies and pies with a colored egg on top. She baked all the Italian delights of the old country that she could not buy at the local IGA market. Everyone who came to visit left with her best creation. Joseph frowned as friends and acquaintances walked out the door with his pies, but Florence replaced them before he became too disgruntled.

At Easter, Joey sat at the kitchen table coloring eggs while his mother prepared the holiday feast. Florence was a good cook and prepared traditional Northern Italian recipes. One favorite family dish was Capozzelli di Angnelli, a lamb's head dressed with seasonings and breadcrumbs. The roasting meat filled the air with delicious scents. Joey's stomach growled. He couldn't wait until the family was sitting around the table passing the scrumptious food around. Florence placed a lamb's head on each person's dish. Joey looked at the food on his plate but held his fork at a safe distance. The eyeballs gave him the creeps.

"Momma," he cried, "it's staring at me."

Everyone laughed and teased him as he ate the tender meat, avoiding the eyes.

"Here, Joey, try the tripe," his sister offered, piling the tasty tips of meat and sauce in his dish.

"I like these," Joey declared as he dug in. When he looked up from his dish, everyone was staring and smiling.

"What?" he asked, searching their faces for the truth behind their secret.

"You just ate sheep stomach," his brother laughed.

Joey began spitting out the remaining food in his mouth, bringing roars of laughter from around the table. Joey's face turned crimson and he smiled sheepishly.

On Thanksgiving, the aroma of cooking turkey kept everyone huddled around the stove. Joey was amazed as he peeked into the oven to see the big bird that was alive just a few hours before. As he walked into the poultry shop with his father, the smell of death hung in the air. The sounds of chickens and turkeys were deafening to his small ears. Peeking into the cages, Joey spotted his turkey. He was the biggest one there.

"That's him," he excitedly told his dad. "I want that turkey."

The holiday crowds caused him to fidget impatiently as he held his father's hand while waiting for their turn. Joey kept looking back at his bird as the people at the front of the line pointed out their choice. "Please don't pick my bird," he said over and over to himself.

Finally, they were standing at the front counter. Joey told the clerk which turkey he wanted. The merchant reached into the cage and grabbed the bird by the neck. He carried it to the back and when he returned, the bird had no feathers and no head.

"Daddy, where is his head?" Joey cried.

Seeing how upset the small boy appeared to be, the merchant quickly offered him some feathers so he could make an Indian headdress. It seemed to satisfy the small boy, but the walk back home was somber as Joey tried to understand that the package under his father's arm was not a pet.

Every Christmas, the children received one toy, but there was plenty of Christmas candy. Joey loved the hard candies that were shaped like a peanut with centers full of peanut butter filling, and he pulled them all out of the dish.

"Joey took all the good ones," his brothers complained.

"Put them back," his father warned.

Joey put back enough to satisfy his siblings but the remainder stayed in his pants pocket, causing an awful mess when his mother pulled them out of the wash. Christmas presents were usually a ball or a sled or a baseball glove and bat. Toys did not require batteries. Kids used their imaginations. One Christmas, Joey's brothers taught him how to make airplanes with their mother's clothespins. They stole their sister's nail polish and painted the wings in the colors of the American flag and some in the colors of the German enemy. Joey loved to express his creativity. He painted his planes with such precision that his brothers were envious.

In September, Joey's family went back to their old neighborhood in Little Italy for the annual San Gennaro Feast to celebrate the Madonna and Italian culture in America. Green, red and white flags littered both sides of the street and the smell of sausage and peppers floated through the air. Sitting on his father's shoulders, Joey had the best seat in the house as he watched the parade go by with the statue of the Blessed Mary.

"Pop," he whispered, "I see a man on that roof with a gun."

"It's okay, Joey. They're just making sure there's no trouble."

Joey was only seven years old and too young to understand the dynamics of his hereditary culture, but his eyes remained wide and innocent as he enjoyed the music and colorful flags. He felt safe with his father.

His father was a tough man, respected and feared as he conducted his business and ran his family. He had friends in high places. Over the years, he gained their trust. In return, Joseph gave them his loyalty. He ventured into various business opportunities, both legal and illegal. You could say he was in the business of making money. Friends like Al Capone and Frankie Vale taught him the art of survival.

Joseph was from Naples and, although he could never be included in the inner circle, he benefited from his Italian heritage. One had to be Sicilian to belong to the untouched and exclusive group that Americans have come to call Mafia. This label was unspoken and unwelcome among Italians who bend the power of the law, using vengeance and quick justice as their trademarks, increasing their powerful grip on New York in the early 1900s. The authorities could not be counted on to solve their problems, so they took it upon themselves and made money by charging local merchants for their protection.

Life was the best it could be, even though the Depression had control of their financial future. The family lived better than most of their neighbors because Joseph would not accept anything less. He did what he had to do to provide for his family.

Joseph became more involved in illegal activities. The money was too good to pass up, and after years in apartments with kerosene heaters and cold water, they finally could afford their own home. It was a two-family brick house with four detached garages lining the back of the house, giving privacy to the long driveway. At the end of the driveway was a small courtyard that led to a back entrance into the finished basement. The wide stairway in the front of the house, with large planters along the sides, led into the main level. A three-bedroom flat at the end of the hallway was located on the left, and a staircase led up to another three-bedroom flat on the second floor. The family now had more space to spread out.

Dolly carried her box of personal items to her bedroom on the first floor with her parents. Joey ran up the stairs, following his brothers to claim their bedrooms. Joey's room was the smallest room, which he jokingly described as "six by eight, without bars," when he grew older. In the hall outside of his room, an iron ladder led up to the roof, where his brothers, Franc and Dom, spent most of their time.

"No, Joey, you are not allowed," they said as they scurried up the ladder. The trap door would close and they were suddenly out of his view. He sat under the door, sucking on the lead soldier that his father helped him mold the night before. Joey knew they were smoking up there, and he imagined they were doing other things they didn't want him to witness.

A True Friend

The feeling has past of being sad,
Wounds do heal of the hurts you had

Few scars do still remain
And memory does still recall the pain

Try to pass the times of being hurt
Be born again as in the moment of birth

The lord has blessed you with the gift of life
With true faith you endure pain and strife

Great the reward, to follow the lords wish
He has shown with faith by the feeding of bread and fish

He is your master, accept no other
Follow his command to love sister and brother

Your body and mind is his to command
For in him only, you will find a true friend

— Gemini Joe

Chapter Three

Joey's siblings were in charge of taking care of him—or losing him. Joey's brothers thought he was spoiled. They loved him in their own distorted way, but abused him by bossing him around and bullying him. Maybe they were trying to toughen little Joey up because he was always sick. Breathing problems made him susceptible to chronic bronchitis. Favored and protected by his mother, father and grandmother, they treated him as if he was going to break. Joey's sister and brothers were expected to show him the same love and attention, but it just inspired resentment. He learned at an early age that attention did not come without a price. Joey was subject to the jealousy of his siblings, especially his twin brothers.

Franc and Dom were always looking for new ways to amuse their devious spirits. Picking on their baby brother was fun, and they never ran out of ideas for torturing him. Under the watchful eye of his mother, Joey felt safe. But when she was not around, he had to watch for his brothers around every corner. He tried to be as quiet as possible, tiptoeing around the apartment so as not to alert them of his presence. Sometimes it was impossible.

Joey stood with his ear pressed against his brothers' bedroom door. He heard them whispering inside and knew that were up to no good. As he cracked the door to take a peek, smoke attacked his eyes and he clumsily closed the door again. He caught his brothers smoking and did not want to face them. Before he could get away, the door swung open and Franc grabbed him.

"Why were you spying on us? You little runt!"

"I wasn't," Joey cried, trying to pry himself from his brother's grip.

"What should we do?" Franc asked Dom.

All at once, Joey found himself hanging upside down out of the second-story window.

"Promise not to tell or we will drop you," Dom screamed.

"I won't tell, I won't tell," Joey promised.

When his brother pulled him back to safety, the room was spinning around. Joey wobbled until he could get his bearings then ran out of the room as fast as his little legs could take him. He could hear his brothers' laughter behind him, but he didn't look back. He learned how to keep a secret, and to stay out of his brothers' path at all costs. Joey never told on them.

Later, Joey and his brother's were examining a dead cat in the alley when they heard their mother call, "Dinner!" into the courtyard.

Dom threw down the stick that he was using to poke the stiff rotting carcass. Franc pushed Joey out of the way to get to the kitchen table before Joey. It was spaghetti night and Franc wanted to be first. Hot steam rose from the dishes of spaghetti and meatballs waiting for the family on the table. Joey was the last to arrive. He looked down at his dish.

"Where's my meatball?" he began to cry. But the kick under the table shut him up. Dom smiled as he shoved Joey's meatball into his mouth. Joey slowly ate the spaghetti on his dish, hoping his mother would notice what happened so that he didn't have to tattle. But by the time his mother finished serving the family and sat down to her own meal, his plate was empty.

"Oh what a good boy you are! You ate all your dinner," she remarked.

Joey just sat there, stomach growling, trying not to look over at his brothers, who were giving him the evil eye.

Franc and Dom were conniving, and the power of the two together was more than Joey could handle. They made their little brother do things for them to avoid getting in trouble, and sometimes they just used him for their amusement.

"Joey, are tears really salty?" Dom asked him one day.

"I don't know," Joey replied.

"Well, if you want to hang around with us, you are going to have to find out," said Franc.

Joey didn't want his brothers to run off without him because they were going to the park a few blocks away, and he wanted them to take him along. "How can I know?" Joey asked.

"Well, there's only one way," Franc said, eyeing Dom. The twins didn't have to use words to know what the other was thinking.

Dom grabbed little Joey while Franc pinched his arms and legs until tears were streaming down his face. "Well?" they asked.

Joey was upset but also amazed. "Yeah, they are salty," he cried and laughed at the same time.

At the beach, Franc and Dom told Joey that they were going to teach him how to swim. Joey was happy his brothers were going to include him so he eagerly followed them down to the shore. Once they were out of parental view, Dom and Franc, grabbed Joey and threw him into the ocean.

"Kick," they yelled, "or you will drown."

He fought for his life to get back to shore, and even though he never trusted his brothers again, he did learn how to swim. After Joey returned to shore, the twins sneaked away and left him alone to play in the sand. Joey was so busy making sand castles that he didn't notice his brothers were gone. As the crowds thinned out at the end of the day, Joey looked around for his brothers. Tears streamed down his face when he realized they left him. A woman noticed that he was alone and crying.

"What's your name, little boy?"

"Joey," he sniffled.

"Are you lost?"

Joey began to cry harder. He realized that Dom and Franc wanted him to be lost.

"Don't cry! I'll take you to the lost and found center for children. They'll find your mommy for you!

Joey didn't want to go. He kept looking back, hoping to see his mother or sister looking for him. The woman took him to the first aid building. She left him in a room with other crying children who could not find their families. Joey worried that no one was going to find him, but soon his mother and sister came through the door, his smiling brothers behind them. He ran to his mom and hugged her tight.

"Don't ever do that again, Joey," she scolded.

"But Dom and Franc," he began then stopped mid-sentence when he noticed Dom's eyes narrow. "Okay, Mommy, I won't get lost again," he promised.

Several days later, after returning from the park, the family came into the house to prepare for dinner. "Where's Joey?" Florence asked her daughter.

"I don't know. Ask Franc and Dom."

Panicked, Joey's parents searched the house then the neighborhood. He had fallen asleep in the back seat of the car and his brothers decided to leave him there. After hours of anguish, his father found him. His mother was so relieved that she showered him with kisses, fueling the jealousy of his brothers. Joey knew that he would pay for the attention.

* * * * * *

The roofs in Brooklyn were places where people went to relax. Similar to country homes where people sat out in their yard, city people set out their lawn chairs on the roof, basking in the summer sun. They planted small trees and vegetable gardens in large pots of soil. Some roofs had coops where families raised chickens or homing pigeons. Once used to relay race results from the Gravesend horse track to the many pool halls in the city, homing pigeons became family pets. It was the bird's turn to race when the racetrack shut down. Members of the pigeon club took pride in the sport, mating their birds and entering the best ones in races. Each bird was fitted with a metal band, engraved with a number that could be read by the meter clocks.

The family discovered empty cages on the roof from the previous owners, and when Joseph brought home a couple of pigeons, he put them in the care of his twin sons. After a few weeks, they came tearing down the iron ladder into the kitchen.

"Two of the birds mated and laid eggs," Dom said.

"They call that a cluster," Franc quickly corrected his brother.

Joey was very curious and wanted to see. "Please let me come up to the roof," he begged.

"Okay, you can look, but you better not touch," Franc warned.

Joey climbed the forbidden ladder and poked his head through the opening in the roof. He stared in amazement at the coop and ran toward the sound of the cooing birds. Fascinated, he watched the mother pigeon sitting on the eggs.

"That's enough," his brother Franc said all too soon, and sent Joey reluctantly back downstairs. Joey could not get the birds out of his thoughts and would sit under the iron stairs, imagining what they were doing up above.

"The eggs are hatching!" his brothers cried several weeks later. The whole family followed Franc and Dom up to the roof. Their father was first. He was not a fat man but husky, and found it hard to squeeze himself up through the small opening. Little Joey was right behind him, not wanting to miss an opportunity to see the birds. His sister, who really didn't care either way, followed them. Their mother stood at the bottom of the iron stairs, hesitant to climb up the ladder.

"Come on," they cried over their shoulders, not stopping to wait for her. When they all disappeared, she hiked up her skirt and began the ascent. Before Joey could run to the coop, Dom grabbed his arm to hold him back. Looking him in the eye, he warned, "Don't you dare touch these birds, do you understand?"

Joey nodded and struggled to get loose. He ran to his father and stayed close as he watched the nest.

Every day, another baby hatched. They were little chirpy things with no feathers and quite ugly. Joey found himself drawn to the roof when his brothers weren't home, sneaking up to have a look at the babies. He knew he was taking a risk, but they were so cute. With one ear on alert for his brothers, he sat inside the coop watching the birds. The last bird that hatched was very tiny. Joey favored him, empathizing since he was in the same predicament in the pecking order.

Against his brother's orders, he carefully took the small bird out of the nest. The bird seemed to love the warmth of his hand as he held him close. Joey felt a special attachment to the baby and wanted to nurture him. He sneaked food to the roof so the bird could eat out of his hand. Then he noticed a big pan filled with water that his brothers put in for the birds to bath in. Joey wanted to give his bird a bath, but the pan was too big. He held the bird in his hand and put it in the water, but thought it wasn't much fun for the bird. Suddenly, he had an idea and ran downstairs to the kitchen. Joey climbed up to the cupboard where his mother kept the china and searched for a saucer the perfect size for a small bird. He ran back up to the roof and filled it with water, then put the little bird in to swim. The bird splashed around, enjoying the bath. Joey decided to call him Splash.

As the birds grew older, his brothers started to plan for the race. The club officials banded and recorded their two eligible birds, one of which was Splash. They were loaded onto a truck with the other birds and driven out to New Jersey. The whole family waited in anticipation for their birds to come home. Within days, each bird came back to the roof. His brothers took the band off and put it in the meter, turning the wheel to record the time. The first bird in was Splash. Franc and Dom jumped up and down.

"We're going to win!" they screamed. They tried to put the bird in the coop, but it refused to go back. Instead, he ran to Joey, who was relieved that he found his way back home.

"Splash!" He yelled, scooping the bird up in his arms.

His brother's eyes fell on him. "What did you do?" Dom screamed. Franc grabbed the bird from his brother and glared at him with squinting eyes. "You're not supposed to make him dependent on humans. You ruined a good bird."

Joey ran behind his mother and peeked out at his angry brothers.

"Leave him alone," his mother proclaimed. In the excitement, his brothers backed off.

After timing the second bird, they rushed off to the Pigeon Club with the meter for the results. Before they climbed down the ladder, Franc turned to his little brother.

"We'll deal with you later."

Joey knew they would, but he was so happy that Splash came home, he didn't care. When he heard Splash came in second and won a blue ribbon, he was so proud. But he knew he would have to be more careful in the future if he wanted to sneak up to the roof.

* * * * * *

The roof was fun, but so was the driveway. Every weekend in the summer, his father set up picnic benches in their driveway. It was Joey's job to bring the dishes, forks and napkins downstairs to set up for dinner. Then he sat on the front steps, waiting impatiently for his brothers to return from fishing on Coney Island.

One Saturday afternoon in June, he finally saw his brothers coming up the street with their buckets and nets, and hoped they had a good catch. When they reached the house, they opened their sacks and dumped the fish onto the sidewalk for their father and brother to see. Joey recoiled when he saw eels squirming around the fish that flopped on the ground. He stood back as his father put them back in the case, then hit the sack on the ground, stunning the eels long enough to cut off their heads. Joey felt sorry for them, but they sure tasted good after his mom cut them into one-inch pieces, sprinkled them with flour, and fried them up for dinner. He loved the way they puffed up when she put them in the hot oil.

Inside the house, a big pot of sauce simmered on the stove, waiting for the water to boil for spaghetti. Out in the driveway, neighbors heard the celebration and walked by with greetings. They knew they would soon be invited to sit at the dinner table.

"Come on in, have some spaghetti," Florence called to them.

As the sun started to set and the daylight dimmed, Joey's father turned on the lights that crisscrossed from the house to the garage. Florence put the radio on the kitchen windowsill so they could listen to music. It was a magical evening as they feasted and laughed around the table. The Italian music played as they sang, ate, and laughed. Joey wished it would never end. Nevertheless, on Sunday night, Joey sadly helped his mother bring all the dishes back upstairs and helped his father put the picnic tables back in the garage until the next week.

* * * * * *

"I want to come," Joey cried as his brothers packed up their fishing gear and bait.

"No, you're too small," Franc said.

Tears welled up in Joey's eyes. "I could help," he insisted.

"What could you do?" Dom began to sneer. "Wait!" His eyes shot toward his twin as an unspoken conversation took place.

"Okay, Joey! You can come, but only if you help carry the gear."

Joey ran up the stairs to tell his mother that he was going fishing. She looked down at his eager face, reluctant to turn him over to his brothers. "Okay, but be careful," she warned.

Joey ran back to his brothers waiting to pile on his burden.

"Come on," they called back to him as he struggled with the bucket and nets.

They took the train to Coney Island and Joey was excited to be included by his older brothers. Joey tried to keep up with them as they walked on the boardwalk toward the pier, but he fell behind. When they realized that it was going to take all day, they ran back and grabbed the rods and bucket.

"A lot of help you are," Franc smirked. He rustled Joey's hair and smiled briefly.

"Come on, before someone gets our spot," Dom impatiently said.

As his brothers hooked the worms, Joey played with the squirming bait, poking them with a stick.

"Can I put the worms on the hook?" he asked Dom.

"No, you stay out of the way or you may get a hook in your eye!"

Joey watched Dom and Franc catch one fish after another. The blood flowed onto the dock as the fish flopped around on the pier. He felt sorry for them and watched in horror as Dom ripped the hook out of the fish's mouth and threw it into the bucket.

He wanted to save the fish, and when he thought his brothers weren't looking, he grabbed one out of the bucket and tossed it back into the sea.

"You can't keep throwing them back!" Franc laughed.

By the end of the day, Joey decided he didn't like fishing. And now that they had fish in the bucket, it was much heavier to carry than when they started out.

"I'll carry the bucket," Dom said, giving Joey the evil eye. "We lost enough fish for one day!"

Memories

In moments when you're sad and blue
And loneliness is worn on you
When bad memories make you think a lot
Perhaps they're best to be forgot

Bring good thoughts to your mind
And to yourself you will be kind
For the mind is deep and memories cruel
To think they sleep, you'd be a fool

Live your life as best you can
Knowing there's a master plan
Learn to live for today
And leave bad memories behind the day

— Gemini Joe

Chapter Four

Growing up in Brooklyn, the children played many outdoor games. Some of their favorites included stoop ball or kick the can, which were similar to soccer and stickball. Stickball, in turn, was similar to baseball. For stickball, a sewer cap in the middle of the street served as home base, and they used chalk to draw the other bases.

Joey's favorite game was marbles, which he played in an empty lot down the street with his friends. In a square box drawn in the dirt, each kid put four marbles in the center. A special marble, called a shooter, shot the other marbles out of the square. The player kept all the marbles he could shoot out, but if the shooter marble stayed in the square, the marbles had to remain; that was the rule. Joey had a steel shooter that Dom gave him.

"No one will have a chance against you with this special marble," Dom told his young brother.

Joey's friends were not happy and complained, "No, Joey, you can't use that marble. You have to use a regular marble or the game is not right." Joey didn't want to cheat, he just wanted to be the best, but he agreed not to use his special marble.

The kids in the neighborhood spent most of their time outside on the streets because something exciting was always happening. The small community was like an extended family. Parents had the security of knowing that their children were safe under the watchful eyes of the neighbors who did not hesitate to report any mischief.

On hot summer days, they sat melting on the pavement, trying to figure out a way to stay cool. If they were lucky, an adult would take mercy on them and open the water main down the street. The kids screamed and yelled as they ran through the flowing water. It didn't take long before the sound of sirens alerted them that fire trucks were coming to re-cap the meter, causing the children to scatter back to their houses.

At home, they waited for the iceman to deliver blocks of ice to each house for their refrigerators. After each delivery, the kids ran behind the truck, trying to get little chips of ice that flew off the back, to cool off. Every time the driver made a stop, some of the kids sneaked around the back and stole the chunks of ice left on the chopping block. The driver knew their tricks and ran after them, yelling, "You kids beat it now or I'll whip you if I catch you!" Dom and Franc were caught more than once and received the harshest punishment: getting kicked in the butt or hit by the iceman's belt. But Joey's cuteness saved him every time. The iceman patted him on the head and told him to run along home before he was hurt.

Every Fourth of July, the streets were closed for a block party. Everyone brought food to set on the long tables lining the sidewalk, and all the grownups sat outside in their chairs. They coached the kids gathering wood for the campfire they would start when the sun went down. Using the flames to light fireworks, they kept watch for the fire department patrolling the neighborhoods to thwart the illegal activity.

Older boys pulled out their stash of firecrackers and cherry bombs from under their beds and the back of their closets. Joey was not allowed to follow his brothers to the corner, but he knew what they were doing with their friends. Dom and Franc carried glass jars with covers, which they intended to use for the explosives, shattering glass and making a loud noise. It was very tricky! You had to be quick to light the cherry bomb and get the cover back before it blew. Sometimes it snuffed out, but most of the time there was enough air in the jar to slowly travel through the wick. Hearing the fire truck, they ran to safety, but before the truck left, the street fire was discovered.

"You're not allowed to start fires in the street," the firemen lectured the adults as they unraveled their hoses to put out the fire.

Soon after the rear lights from the fire truck disappeared, the fire blazed once more and smoldering embers glowed in the dark of night. Joey smiled as he waved the lit sparkler his dad handed him. At the bottom of the fire were potatoes or "mickies," named for the Irish, who introduced potatoes in America. Attached to wire hangers, the potatoes lined the bottom of the woodpile. As the fire blazed, the potatoes cooked in the inferno. Late at night, when the wood was almost gone, the mickies were removed from the dying fires. They were hard and black on the outside, but white and fluffy on the inside. Joey watched his father unravel the foil and split his potato.

"Here you go, Joey," his father proudly said as he handed him the prize.

Joey lobbed on the butter and sprinkled salt on top, before he dug his folk into the white fluffy potato, avoiding the black charred skin.

"This is delicious," he beamed to his dad.

The days began to get shorter, and summer was drawing to an end. Soon it would get dark early and the sound of playing children would have to be taken indoors. Joey savored each remaining day in the sun.

* * * * * *

Dolly stayed as far away from her brothers as she could. She didn't want to get in the middle of all their fighting, and was no help to her baby brother when the twins got hold of Joey. Besides, she had better things to do with her time. She had quite a large circle of friends and a string of boyfriends, which she paraded past her family on a daily basis. All of Dolly's boyfriends respected her to keep from getting on her father's bad side. They knew he was a powerful man with ties in the community. Dolly basked in his notoriety. A mafia princess, she was "daddy's little girl" and did not find it hard to get what she wanted from him.

Joey loved his sister but he modeled himself after his older brothers. He wanted to be tough like them, but when he was alone, he did not feel so tough. They had each other, but he was eight years younger and felt left out of their plots and schemes.

Joey inherited all his brothers' hand-me-down clothes. Most of them were old and worn, and some were too big. When the weather began to get cold, his mom insisted that he put on a sweater before he left for school. The sleeves were too long with holes in the elbows. Joey did not want to wear it and cried that all the children were going to laugh at him. But arguing just made his mother angry, so he slowly walked to school, wiping his tears and runny nose on the sleeves that slid back down over his hands. He realized that they came in handy and began to have an idea. He showed the kids his holey sweater before they noticed it, to make it seem funny. When he walked into his class, he ran up to the first group of students he saw and said, "Hey guys, look at this sweater, it has holes and I could pull my hands up and stick my fingers out." It worked like a charm. Everyone laughed, and Joey laughed along with the group, but in his heart, he was still crying. He wished that he was the older brother and handed down his clothes to Dom and Franc.

Dom wasn't as mean as Franc when he was alone. Joey thought it was because he lost one of his eyes when he was thirteen, while chopping wood. Winter wood burners in Brooklyn were continuously hungry for fuel and Dom wanted to make some money selling firewood. He went door to door to get orders, and then rushed back to his chopping block when he had a sale. In his haste, he became careless and a splinter of wood shot into his eye. At the hospital, his mother cried as the doctor told the family that Dom's eye was gone. He was fitted with a glass eye and from that day on, he didn't act tough. Franc appointed himself protector of his other half and became meaner.

Everyone in the neighborhood knew Dom and Franc as "the twinnies." No one dared to mess with them since they were the bullies of the schoolyard. They were not the only mean brothers around and had many friends with younger siblings. This group of older boys met in the park often, toting their little brothers, who had no choice in the matter. They put fighting mitts on the younger boys and pitted them against each other in a ring made with chalk. It was serious business as they put their bets down on the winner.

Franc whispered in Joey's ear, "You better win."

One day, Joey found himself staring across from a friend from his third grade class. He had one minute to decide what to do as he blocked everything out of his mind. He lunged toward the boy and hit him with everything he had. The boy looked amazed, since they were friends and liked each other before this moment. Then he began hitting back, which only made it worse.

Joey whispered to his friend, "Go down. Go down."

But the boy feared his own older brother and refused to quit right away. Joey squinted his eyes and began to hit harder and faster. Finally, the boy went down and Joey could hear his brothers yelling with joy. Unfortunately, he fought so well that his brothers challenged everybody, big and small. He could not let down his guard so Joey learned to fight for his life.

His brothers did a good job of toughening him up and Joey grew up fast, becoming street smart beyond his years. At the age of eleven, Joey took his daily walk to the candy store. A penny made his hand sweat and he switched it from left to right. With his head not quite reaching the counter, he lifted himself up on his toes.

"One cigarette please," he said to the merchant.

"That will be one cent, little guy, and here are your two matches."

Smoking seemed natural for Joey. His father smoked, and so did his brothers. He didn't like it at first, but was determined to get use to it, and the quest for tobacco caused him to sneak cigarettes and hunt for unwanted pennies. That first cigarette turned into a three-pack-a-day habit.

* * * * * *

At school, Joey was free to express his creativity in drawings and paintings, and the teachers loved his work. He was not sure where this talent came from, but decided it must have been from his uncle, who was discovered by an agent in Hollywood and was asked to create all the cave scenery in movies about Huckleberry Finn and Injun Joe.

During the holidays, he was always asked to come down to the principal's office and draw pictures of snowflakes, snowmen, Santa and his elves, sleds and reindeer for all the windows. He burst with pride, knowing he had true talent, and continued to draw throughout his life as a source of comfort and an escape from the cruelties of his world.

After a long, cold winter, spring renewed the spirit of learning and school became fun again. The teacher told everyone to wear his or her sneakers to school for a race. Joey had a problem. He did not own sneakers. As he walked home, he tried to figure out what he was going to do. He remembered that his brother had an old pair of sneakers. He ran the rest of the way home and searched high and low. Finally he found a sad looking pair of sneakers hidden in the back of the closet. One of the laces was shorter than the other, and was tied together by a knot. Joey pushed his feet into them. They were a little big, but he laced up the one good shoe and tried them out by running down the street. They kept falling off and Joey couldn't run quickly.

"This won't work," he said aloud. "I will lose the race." He ran back inside to find his dad. "Dad, these shoes are too big for me. What should I do?"

Joey's father looked at the oversized sneakers and had an idea. He stuffed some old socks in the toe end of them and told his son to try it again. This time, the sneakers did not fall off and Joey could to run plenty fast. He smiled at his father, who could figure out any problem.

The next day at school, the teacher brought the whole class into the schoolyard. "We are going to have a race," she announced. Joey was determined to win. He looked at the faces of his fellow classmates, who also wanted to win. Getting into a ready stance, he attentively waited for the teacher to blow the whistle. He was off to a great start, but his left sneaker flew off his foot. Joey fell to the ground, watching the other boys run past him. He felt humiliated when they pointed and laughed at him. That night, his father promised to buy him a new pair of sneakers, "The best that money could buy." But it was too late. Joey lost his chance to prove himself and no longer had a desire to race.

* * * * * *

On a warm Saturday morning, Joey heard his father getting ready to run some errands. He quickly jumped out of bed and into his clothes, running into the kitchen with only one leg in his pants.

"Pop, can I come?" Joey begged.

Joseph looked down at his son. "Only if you promise to use both legs," he laughed.

Walking on Eighteenth Avenue with shops lined up on either side of the street, Joey and his father stopped in the bakery and Joey's father bought him a cookie. They passed an ice cream store and Joey's father bought him an ice cream cone. They passed a candy store and his father bought him some chocolate. Then they came to a new tropical fish store and decided to go look inside. Joey could not get enough of the colorful fish in the tanks. He was particularly interested in one tank with beautiful beta fish which were isolated from each other by glass partitions.

"Why are those fish alone?" Joey asked his father.

"Those are Chinese warrior fish," his father said. "If you put them together, they will fight to the death."

"How do they have babies?" Joey's curiosity was evident in his wide eyes that remained glued to the fish.

Joseph looked at his son and said, "Why don't we find out?" To Joey's surprise and delight, his father bought a tank, supplies and two fish, one male and one female.

The fish in Joey's room attracted his brothers, who sat with him on the bed to watch the fish swim back and forth, mesmerized by the sound of the bubbles. They noticed the fish bumping into the glass partition that separated them.

"They want to mate," an excited Franc declared. He was always smart when it came to animals. They lifted the glass just long enough for the fish to mate, then put the partition back and waited. It wasn't long before the female laid her eggs. The female began eating the eggs on her side but they managed to save half. Quickly, they removed the female and watched as the male collected the eggs and put them in a bubble. They met in Joey's room everyday to check if the eggs were hatched. For once, Joey was the boss and his brother's were nice to him so he would let them in his room.

"Look," Dom yelled, as they stared into the tank. A small flick rose from the eggs and floated to the top, then another, and another. The eggs were hatching, but before they could get a good look, the father fish ate one.

"Oh, no!" Dom jumped up. "We have to get them out quick!"

They separated the babies and watched as they grew everyday. When they were big enough, Joey brought them back to the fish store, where he received fifty cents for each fighter fish. A new business venture hatched.

When Joey tired of the fish, he gave them to Franc. Joey turned his attention to horses. He loved them more than pigeons or fish. A picture book filled with wild horses and racing horses sat on the shelf alongside nine horse statues in his room. Every time Joey bought a new horse, Franc was right there admiring it. The two brothers developed a bond through animals that reinforced the power of family.

When Joey lost interest, Franc picked up new horses from time to time to add to their collection. Joey saw how much his brother loved the collection, so he gave them all to Franc. His brother built a showcase with mirrors, glass and lights to display the two hundred horses they had collected through the years. Later, Joey regretted giving away his collection but he didn't think he could have displayed them as well as his older brother.

When Joey turned twelve years old, he wanted to do something to make money. Dom said, "I will build you a shoeshine box and you could shine shoes, but I want half of your earnings."

Joey agreed, so Dom built the shoeshine box. It was made of lousy wood. The nails weren't too good either, some went in and some of them bent. Joey invested the last of his savings to buy brushes and polish. His brother instructed him to take the train to Coney Island and charge a nickel for each shine. When Joey entered the train station, he had no money. It was a nickel to get on the train. As Joey stood thinking, he watched as two customers put one nickel in the turnstile and pushed through together. He waited for someone to let him squeeze through. A woman with many packages fumbled for her coin at the turnstile.

"Can I squeeze in with you?" Joey asked.

"No, go find your mother," she angrily scolded.

Joey backed away. He waited for the next person to come. It was a man, not as old as his father, but older than his brothers.

He studied his face, trying to decide if it was safe to ask, but before he could, the man offered.

"Do you need to ride the train?"

Joey did not speak, but nodded his head.

"Well, get in front of me and I'll let you through, but hurry so we don't get caught."

Joey squeezed in to the other side.

"Thanks, mister," he said.

Together, they waited for the next train. He heard the roar coming down the tracks, and jumped on as soon as the door opened. He took a seat on the opposite end of the man and looked out of the window, not wanting to miss his stop. Joey felt grown up sitting on the train by himself.

When he came out of the train station, he set up his shoeshine box on the corner and sat down. The colors, lights and music along the busy fairway made him feel like he was in a magical world. He could hear the roar of The Cyclone off in the distance, and even though he had no money to ride the famous roller coaster, he could feel the sensation of the downward drop by the sounds of the screaming riders. Just as he was starting to get comfortable, two young boys came and stood in front of his box.

"This is our corner," they yelled, grabbing his box and throwing it in the street. As Joey jumped up to save his homemade shoeshine box, they shoved him to the ground. Stunned by their anger, Joey packed up his stuff and waited for a train ride home. This time, he slipped in under the turnstile. It was easy because commuters were on their way home from work and the station was crowded. When he arrived home, he told his brothers what happened.

"You go back tomorrow and get your spot or we will kick the shit out of you!" they yelled.

Joey thought for a while. Either his brothers were going to do him in or the two boys would. He decided to give it another try. As fortune would have it, there was only one brother waiting on the corner the next day. "Didn't my brother tell you this is our corner?"

"I'm not leaving because my brothers will be mad," Joey said.

"Well," the other boy said, "I guess you can stay, but don't take our customers."

Joey smiled to himself as he set up his station. His first customer thought he did such a good job that he gave him a quarter. The next customer had black shoes with white socks. Joe tried really hard, but some of the polish rubbed off on his socks. The man was so mad that he refused to pay for the shine. He even claimed he was a cop, threatening that he could arrest Joey if he felt like it. After that, Joey was more careful. At the end of the day, he left with a pocket full of nickels and one quarter. Joey had a happy feeling throughout the train ride home as he pressed his face to the window, calculating all the corners he could use to set up his new business.

Janet Sierzant

Games of Play

See the happy girls and boys
Playing with their colorful toys
Hear them counting one and one is two
Learning colors, orange, red and blue

Merrily they dance and sing a song,
All moms and dads should sing along
For no better time to enjoy
As when they're young and gay

Join in all their songs and games
And take the time to play
For this time and hour will surely pass
And when you look they're grown at last

Ready to leave with nobility and pride
Cherish those moments, that magical ride
Lessons are learned and then one day
They will remember you shared in their games of play

— Gemini Joe

Chapter Five

Joey and his brothers walked to school every morning. School provided Joey the opportunity to express his creative side. He wasn't very good at his studies but excelled in anything artistic. Graded on his artwork instead of arithmetic or reading, Joey didn't think the teachers did him any favors, and he always knew it deep inside. Sometimes he felt like he was set apart from the other kids. He despised this because he wanted to be like the other boys. He was embarrassed when the teacher made the students vote for a captain of the class to keep them in control whenever she had to leave the room. Voted captain by most of the girls, Joey feared that the other boys in the class would think he was a sissy.

He tried extra hard to prove himself in the schoolyard during recess. In the back of the school, all the kids climbed on a cement wall. Joey watched as two boys stood on the five-foot wall and pushed each other until one fell off. He recognized one of them. Jimmy was a hall monitor just like Joey, but they never spoke to each other. "I'm king of the mountain," Jimmy yelled as he danced on the ledge, ready to take on the next challenger. When he noticed Joey standing on the side, Jimmy jumped off and leapt onto Joey's back. Flipping through the air, Jimmy found himself looking up at the sky. Joey smiled and jumped onto the wall to take Jimmy's place. "Now I'm king of the mountain," he yelled.

Jimmy jumped up to take on the challenge. Joey moved in the direction of his opponent and pushed against him, forcing Jimmy to fall off the wall. Joey remained "king of the mountain," for a while, anyway. The two boys challenged each other everyday in the schoolyard, until one day, they began to sit together during lunch. Joey found his new best friend.

Jimmy and Joey patrolled the halls of their school as class monitors. Because they were left back so many times, they were older than the other children at the school. The teachers put them in charge of making sure no one cut class or walked off the school premises. Mostly, they directed the young children to their classes. After discovering that they only lived a couple of blocks from each other, they started wandering from their homes to explore the neighborhood. They also found that they could cut school without attracting too much attention. Together they explored their community as they ventured further from home.

During the Depression, crime rose in proportion to unemployment in the city. Desperation tested the honor of some. Those who had no tolerance for humbling themselves turned to illegal means. Even children accepted crime as an alternative to being hungry. One summer day they discovered a farm. It stretched for the length of a whole block and was surrounded by a brick wall. Joey and Jimmy could see the fruit-laden trees behind the "fortress."

"We need to come back when it starts to get dark," Jimmy said.

"Okay, I'll meet you back in this spot when the sun goes down," Joey promised.

As the sun sank deep in the sky, both boys stood looking up at the wall.

"Get on my shoulders," Joey instructed his friend.

When Jimmy hoisted himself on top of the wall, he braced himself and stretched out his arm. "Hold on to me and climb," he told Joey.

Joey reached out for his friend and trusted that he would not drop him as he wedged his shoe in a crack and made his way up. Finally at the top, both boys laughed before they jumped down to the other side. They scrambled up the nearest tree. It was a peach tree and the sweet, fragrant scent intoxicated them. They began picking the most beautiful, ripe peaches they had ever seen. Fruit like this was a luxury and it was rarely seen at their dinner tables. Jimmy picked so many that he began to lose his grip on them. They kept tumbling down to the earth and splattering on the old tree's roots.

"Put them in your shirt," Joey whispered." Hurry! Let's get out of here before we get caught."

It was easier getting back over the wall because the shrubbery along the wall gave them an extra boost, but jumping with the heavy peaches in their shirts caused them to lose their balance. Both boys landed on their stomachs, or rather, on the peaches that were tucked under their shirts against their stomachs. Some of the peaches broke open against their chests as the weight of their bodies crushed the soft fruit.

The boys ran to Joey's house, but by the time they arrived, both boys were pulling the fruit out and throwing it on the ground. They lost interest in their catch because they were too busy scratching. The fur from the peaches rubbed into their skin, causing red patches and uncontrollable itching. They raced into the bathroom, ripping off their shirts and trying to get to the cold water in the tap.

"You guys are so stupid!" Joey's brothers laughed and howled. By the time they cooled off, it was time for Jimmy to go home. They could not see if any of the peaches made it through the ordeal because it was too dark. But the next morning, they discovered that none of the fruit was intact. They decided that it was not worth the trouble, and the next time they passed the farm, they kept walking.

* * * * * *

Joey, Jimmy and their friend Tony stood under a street light, smoking a cigarette Jimmy stole from his father.

"What's that noise?" Jimmy asked.

"It's my stomach," Tony grimaced. "I'm starving."

Joey smiled. "I have an idea," he yelled, as he stamped out the butt. "Follow me, but you have to be very quiet." He led his friends down an alley. They could see lights in the apartment windows above. Joey pointed to one that was not lit, and put his finger to his lips before he climbed the fire escape. He opened the box that sat on the balcony and quickly rummaged through it, pulling out items and tucking them into his jacket. When he jumped down, he produced a block of cheese, some jam and a carton of milk. They divided the feast, and then looked up to find another food source.

This time, they all participated. Just as Tony was about to climb down the ladder, a light blinded his eyes. He dropped to the ground and ran down the alley as a man yelled out, "Who's there?"

Once he caught up with his friends under the streetlight, Tony heaved, trying to catch his breath. Joe and Jimmy laughed so hard that they almost forgot about their treasures.

They pulled the food out of their coats and placed it on the curb.

"Hey, Jimmy, what is that you are holding aside?"

"It's mine," he said protectively, holding the bottle he refused to share.

"Oh, he has prune juice," Tony yelled. "Give us some."

"No, it's mine. I'll share everything, except this."

"Some friend you are," Joey and Tony said, their mouths watering for the rare juice as they watched Jimmy chug it down.

Just as he was draining the last drop from the bottle, they heard the sirens of a police car that was heading toward them, lights flashing. Before they could scramble, the cops were jumping out of their vehicle, grabbing Tony by the collar. "What are you kids up to? And where did you get this food?"

"It's ours," Jimmy claimed.

"You kids need to get out of here. Where do you live? Never mind. You," he said to Joey. "You go that way," he pointed down the street. He then turned to Jimmy and pointed him in the opposite direction. Still holding onto Tony, he shoved him in the back of his car. "I know where you live," he sneered.

The next day, Tony was at Joey's door. "My father really whipped me good!" he complained, rubbing his backside. "What happened to Jimmy?"

"I don't know," Joey said. "Let's go check on him."

Jimmy's mother answered the door. "I'm sorry, guys, but Jimmy won't be coming out today. He's sick."

Joey and Tony headed toward the park to spy on the local gangs. It felt strange to be there without Jimmy. He would never miss an opportunity to get out of his house.

The next day, the two boys went back to their friend's house. Once more, Jimmy's mother came to the door and sent them away. "I wonder what's wrong with him," Joey said.

"I don't know, but whatever it is, I hope we don't get it!" Tony replied.

By the third day, they insisted on answers. Before Jimmy's mother closed the day, Joey spoke out.

"What's wrong with him?" he asked.

"He must have eaten something bad. He can't get off the toilet," his mother admitted.

Tony started to laugh, but Joey pinched him, and he let out a scream instead. Joey waited until they were halfway down the block before a fit of laughter escaped him. Both boys were rolling around holding their sides from the comedic irony of the situation.

"It was the juice," Tony yelled.

"Yeah, that'll teach him not to share," Joey laughed.

The next time they saw Jimmy, he had clearly lost some weight.

"Hey, guys," he said, as if he had never disappeared.

Tony smirked, "Hey, Prunes."

"Prunes!" Joey bellowed. "That's great, Tony. From now on, that's what we'll call him."

* * * * * *

Joey could hear Prunes coming from two blocks away. Their special whistle sounded the signal, and each was trained to listen for the tone.

Joey noticed that Prunes looked excited as he took long strides down the street toward him.

"What's wrong?" Joey yelled out before the two teenage boys were face to face.

"We need to meet the guys down at the park," Prunes instructed. "Marty got beat up last night, and we're gonna teach those Spics a lesson."

Joey's head began to spin. He saw plenty of fighting at home and hated confrontation.

"Maybe he was somewhere that he shouldn't have been," Joey tried to convince him. "Why do we have to get into it?"

"Because we are friends, and friends look out for each other," Prunes snapped, as he stared at his best friend.

"Okay," Joey gave in, and the two of them began to head toward the park.

Marty was waiting along with his brother Sal and his friend Flip

"We need to get those guys," Marty said as he paced back and forth in front of the cement park table.

Flip was sitting on the edge of the table smoking a cigarette with a smile on his face. Nothing ever fazed him and his mood was always upbeat, even in times of trouble. His walk often turned into a bop as he went down the street. He would flip up his feet to one side, and then continue walking, amusing himself and annoying his friends. His real name was Phil, but they nicknamed him Flip.

"Okay, let's go," Sal said when Joe and Prunes joined them.

It was a time of turf wars. Danger waited around every corner if you were alone on someone else's territory. Joey did not like to fight, not unless he had a few drinks in him. His father must have gotten wise that his liquor was disappearing and hid it, because it had been two months since Joey had had a drink. Joey was only fourteen, but he already had a taste for scotch. But at this moment, he was sober as a priest and feeling scared.

The five boys strode down the street, pumping each other up for a fight. Joey tried to hide his fear, but Prunes could see through this façade.

"What's the matter, Joey? Are you scared?"

"No! Not at all," Joey replied. "I just think we need some kind of weapon, that's all! Maybe we could find a stick or a belt of some sort."

The opposition spotted them coming down the street and knew what was in store. Before Joey knew it, fists were flying and blood was spattering as the two gangs stood their ground. Fear took over his legs and he ran to the parking lot, searching for a weapon. The fight ended before Joey returned with an antenna that he ripped off a parked car.

"What are you going to do with that?" Prunes laughed.

"I was going to beat them off," he grinned, but he was glad that he didn't have to use it.

******

Joey and his friends sat in front of his house watching the cars go by. It was the middle of August and their summer vacation had lost some of its luster. They fished, swam, played ball, hung out in the park and explored their neighborhood until they couldn't think of any thing else to do. Jimmy bounced a ball mindlessly, trying to hit the edge of the curb so it would bounce back at him. The ball hit Tony in the head.

"Ouch," Tony shouted, jumping up ready to fight.

"Come on guys, knock it off," Joey warned.

"I'm bored. What do you want to do?" Tony asked.

"I don't know. Maybe we should go down to the beach," Jimmy suggested.

"Nah! I don't want to...Hey, wait. I have an idea," Joey's face lit up. "Let's build a boat."

"Yeah," they yelled and jumped up, ready to get to work.

"My father has old wood in the back. I'm sure he won't mind if we use it," Joey offered.

The saw buzzed and the hammer swung, making a racket the whole neighborhood could hear. Dom came upon them as they worked.

"What the hell are you guys doing?" he asked with disdain.

"We're building a boat."

Dom stood with a smirk planted firmly on his face, but he did not leave. He stayed to watch with interest.

"We need to do this in the basement," Joey said. "Winter is coming and we will have plenty of heat and light inside." Joey looked at his friends to see a sign of approval. They thought this was a good idea. The four boys carried the material down to the basement. Joey, Tony, and Jimmy worked hard. When the boat was finished, two boys grabbed the front and two grabbed the back as they lifted the heavy vessel and moved toward the door.

"What the hell!" Dom yelled. "It's too big! You idiots forgot to measure the doorway." His face began to turn crimson. He dropped his side of the boat and ran up the stairs. "I can't believe I wasted my goddamn time with you sons of bitches!"

Joey and his friends looked down at their boat in silence. The seat in the center made the boat arch and it was too wide for the doorway.

"What do we do now?" they asked, looking to Joey for the answer. Joey was quiet. He was thinking hard. Excitement grew as they saw the light in his eyes ignite. Joey went to work, removing the seat. "Prunes, you and Tony grab the back, I'll get the front." Together they squeezed the boat out the door.

Dom was outside puffing on a cigarette. When he saw them, he did a double take. "How the hell did you do that?"

Joey smiled and bragged how he figured out a solution to the dilemma.

"Damn it, Joey, I could have told you to do that," his brother said. They all laughed until their sides hurt.

The summer seemed short, and soon it was time to go back to school. Jimmy managed to graduate to the seventh grade, but

Joey was not so lucky. Once again, he was left back. This time, he did not have his friend to help pass the time or cut school with. Embarrassed to be the oldest kid in his sixth grade class, he stopped going. His mother was at work all day and his father didn't care.

In the morning, Joey heard a knock on the front door. He rolled over and tried to get back to sleep but the voices in the kitchen prevented his slumber. One of them sounded familiar. Curiosity caused him to get up, and he quickly put on his pants and walked into the kitchen.

"If the boy doesn't want to go to school, it's all right with me."

"But Mr. Fuccino, Joey needs an education," the principal argued.

Joey could not believe his eyes. He saw his teacher and the principal in deep conversation with his father.

"What he needs is a job," his father snapped.

Seeing Joey enter the room, his teacher became braver.

"Your son has great talent," she said. "There is an alternative school where he can develop his artistic abilities. He is a very good artist, you know," she quickly added, hoping pride would make him change his mind.

Joey's eyes opened wide. He loved the idea.

"I'm not wasting my money on some art school," his father barked. "He needs to learn something useful so he can make a living."

"But, Mr. Fuccino," the principal said, "surely we could work something out."

"No, you are wasting my time," Joseph said, as he closed his mind and herded them to the door.

Joey was crushed. He packed up his art supplies and tucked them under his bed, refusing to draw for awhile. He did not let his father know how disappointed he was, and acted like he didn't care.

A Silent Tear

The Waterfall announces a deep loud roar
A desire to be heard
Each person's life holds deep pain
And as the years go by
The pain is greatest, always wishing
to return to the top of the waterfall

Time takes hold of the body soul and mind
Wanting again that moment of life where it began
For the beginning is as the end
At birth a loud cry for life and
At the end a silent tear

— Gemini Joe

Chapter Six

Beneath the veil of family and enterprise, Joseph did all right for himself. A laundry route was the perfect cover for his real occupation. His sons helped haul the clean and dirty clothes while he conducted his business. Some of the tenements in Brooklyn had four or five flights of stairs, and it seemed like the heaviest loads had to go to the top. Joseph only took the lower floors, leaving his sons to climb the floors above. With a cigarette dangling from his lips, he said, "I'll get this one."

Years of smoking caused Joseph to cough and lose his breath. The fact that he had emphysema didn't stop him from smoking two packs a day. Young Joey watched with disgust as his father coughed and spit along the sidewalk.

"Please, Pop, don't smoke."

"Shut your mouth and deliver that sack," his father said in a low stern voice.

Realizing he had overstepped, Joey quickly tried to make his father laugh by imitating one of their customers. Joseph looked at his son through narrowed eyes, then smiled, letting his anger melt away. "Let's get back to work now, Joey."

From one apartment to another, they picked up dirty laundry and delivered clean bundles, folded and wrapped in brown paper tied with string. It was hard work and most of it fell on Joey. His twin brothers distracted each other and didn't get much done.

The laundry route brought in a small salary, but the real money came in from under the table. Everyone knew about Joseph's ties to the Mob, and his duties as a bookie inflated his notoriety in the neighborhood as he made his rounds to collect his money. Whispers were kept out of earshot as he walked past the people on the street. They respectfully greeted him but were careful to avoid eye contact. In his little black book, he recorded the names, horses and amounts wagered for each race. Each wager was no less than two dollars per race and his book was full of names and numbers. Betting on horses was a popular activity, and everyone wanted to win. Joey loved horses, but he knew that something sinister was going on. No one told him that his father was doing something illegal, but the hushed voices and whispers among his father's friends kept him from asking questions.

Puzzled by his father's joy on their way to pay off his lucky clients, Joey looked up at his father. "Pop, why are you so happy? They won! Aren't you going to lose money?"

"No, son. People get greedy when they win. Next time, that guy will bet four dollars."

"Oh," Joey absently replied as a flash of disappointment shot through his young mind. He wanted to think his father was a good man, but something gnawed at him.

Taking money from people didn't cause Joseph to blink twice. They obviously had a gambling problem and it was not up to him to fix them. He preferred to think of it as a sin tax. No one forced them to bet. The only time his conscious rose was when he had to take money from a woman.

"Please, lady, don't put your money on this horse. I don't think he's going to win," he warned. Undeterred, she would insist on placing her bet. Joey watched his father struggle with the decision to take her money. They continued down the street in silence after Joseph failed to persuade her. The next day, he often returned to give her back some of the money she lost.

"Go buy your children some shoes, and be more careful with your money," he scolded.

Joey felt proud of his father when the lady kissed and thanked him for his generosity. Joey preferred to focus on the acts of kindness he witnessed from his father. He dismissed the methods used by his father to earn his money, convincing himself that he was a good man. Joseph could afford to be generous. Placing wagers on fixed races made him a lot of money.

Joseph was a heavy smoker. He especially had a hard time in the morning, when he coughed for hours trying to clear his lungs. He needed to put money on a horse race early that morning, but he was not feeling well. He though he was alone in the house, then noticed that fourteen-year-old Joey was still in bed.

"Get up and make yourself useful," he yelled into Joey's room.

Joey got out of bed and went into the kitchen where his father was coughing into the sink.

"What do you need, Pop?"

"Take this bag and go down to the track. Go to window six, only window six. Then take the bag and go to Pennsylvania Avenue. There will be a car waiting."

Joey felt important. He was happy to fill in for his father. Dressed in his finest Sunday clothes and carrying a brown lunch bag, Joey stepped up to the designated window at Belmont Race Track. Pushing the bag under the glass partition, he took a step back and looked around, making sure not to attract suspicion. The clerk knew that the stack of bills inside were not for the boy standing in front of him. Agreements with crooked jockeys or people behind the scenes made the odds of coming in first place a sure bet. The clerk gave Joey more tickets than the maximum allowed, stuffing them back into his bag.

Joey approached the long, black limousine parked in the shadows of the empty lot. He nervously jumped into the back seat as the door opened. Stale tobacco and alcohol invaded his nose and cigar smoke made his eyes sting.

"So, you're Joseph's son," the voice in the front seat declared with interest. "Do you have something for me?"

The mysterious man waited impatiently as Joey fumbled in his coat pocket for the bag of racing tickets. He handed them to the man in the front seat, but before he could pull his arm back, the man grabbed him. "Who do you think you are, Joey? John Gody! Next time, lose the suit."

"Yes, sir," Joey respectfully replied before leaving with a fifty dollar bill and a smile.

* * * * * *

Prohibition had provided new opportunities to make money, because it was hard to enforce in New York. While the Navy tried to keep watch on the harbors, they were ineffective at patrolling the northern borders. Trucks rolled into the city every day with fresh supplies, and the underground economy boomed. The sound of smashing bottles became a daily occurrence as police stormed into warehouses suspected of storing liquor.

Mayor La Guardia, elected to clean up the widespread corruption in New York, was originally against Prohibition, but the law was the law, and he was required to lead the daily raids. During the week he fought the crime waves of the city, but on Saturdays he took the day off to read comics on the radio to the children of New York. Mayor La Guardia was a hero in Joey's eyes, and he loved the mayor's humor and calming voice.

Joseph was the captain in charge of the liquor smuggled in from Canada. He made deliveries to local speakeasies and collected the profits. It was risky, but he had the protection of his friends, all of whom had a few law enforcement buddies in their pockets.

While he was arrested at least once a month, Joseph knew this was just a formality. Well paid, the police turned a blind eye toward certain criminals. "Joseph, we're going to have to take you down to the station," the chief of police would wink.

It wasn't long before bail was made from someone, and Joseph was home in time for dinner. Prohibition shifted the distribution of power, making some people rich, but the average, law-abiding citizens didn't have a chance.

Not many people know the history of the seven Sicilian brothers, banished from their country for refusing to pay the king. Forced to live in the woods among the criminals, murderers and thieves, they banded together for survival. Tough and loyal, they formed an alliance that stood the test of time and reached across the ocean to the new Land of Opportunity. When local authorities would not solve their problems, they took it upon themselves to protect each other and preserve their heritage through an alliance known as the Mafia, or Cosa Nostra in Sicily. Each cosa or clan clams sovereignty over a specific territory. Inside thugs with the authority of their bosses dealt with the oppressors by constructing cement shoes and dumping the evidence in the sea. Those seeking to avoid problems sought out the Mafia's services, but there was always a price. Merchants paid the weekly five dollars to the Mob for protection. Not all were happy about this arrangement, but they knew what would happen if they spoke out. Those who refused were soon out of business, with no explanation and no redress. Corruption outweighed the good intentions of the organization formed to take care of their own, and their reputation for violence instilled fear in the community. In an attempt to do damage control, the Mob opened soup kitchens for the poor. This made them look benevolent to most people and, ironically, gave them protection by keeping them in good standing in the community.

Once Prohibition ended, the country faced a depression that put a hardship on the people who tried to survive in the city. During these times, there was a lot of money to be made if you had the stomach for it, and Joseph Fuccino always did. His illegal activities brought in more money than the family needed. Joey often wondered where all this money was coming from, but quickly dismissed the thought, preferring to think of his father as successful. Those who feared the law relied on meager wages for physical labor. They barely kept food on the table. More often than not, they found themselves in a financial pinch and paid a visit to the man who could bail them out. Joseph never intended to be a loan shark, but found it easier than transporting liquor. Calling in loans kept Joseph hitting the pavement to collect his payments, interest and fees in spite of his breathing problems. He never refused a loan, even when it was more money than he could lend. He made a connection in Chicago for back up, and gladly gave the loan request to someone above, taking a smaller cut of the interest.

Joseph held his meetings in public places, such as local bars or pool halls, but preferred his favorite Italian restaurant. As the hostess seated Joseph at his reserved table, the waiter followed close behind to take his order.

"Good evening, Mr. Durante," Joseph greeted the waiter.

"Please, call me Jimmy," the young man with an unusually large nose replied.

Joseph looked over at the bandstand and asked his waiter, "Are you planning to sing at this restaurant forever, Jimmy?"

"No sir, I want to make records and become famous. My friend, Al, started here and now he is now well known in the music world," replied the excited singing waiter.

"Keep up the good work, Jimmy, and make sure you sing my favorites tonight." Joseph stuffed a large bill in the boy's vest pocket.

"Yes, sir," Jimmy replied.

Joseph ordered a scotch and an appetizer of clams on the half-shell and waited for his contact to arrive.

"Pauly!" He waved across the room to the short, burly man scanning the restaurant.

Paul walked to the table and took a seat, laying his briefcase on the table. Joseph waved the waiter over to their table and instructed him to take his companion's order.

"What would you like?" Joseph asked. "Order whatever you want. It's on me."

Paul was not shy. He ordered a vodka straight up and oysters for an appetizer. Then he requested a steak, cooked medium rare. Joseph ordered fettuccini alfredo, something his wife refused to make for him because of his weight.

Paul opened his case and pulled out a list of customers for Joseph to examine.

"You need to pay these people a visit, Joseph. Convince them that it would be in their best health to pay what they owe."

"No problem, Pauly! I'll get started first thing tomorrow."

"You'll get started first thing tonight," Paul replied, gulping down his drink and slamming the glass down on the table.

"Okay, tonight. I will visit them tonight," Joseph said, trying not to show he was out of breath. He noticed that Paul's nose was crooked and decided that must be the reason for his discontent.

* * * * * *

When Joseph's emphysema prevented him from making his rounds, he had to rely on others to collect his earnings. He thought they were low-quality people and did not want them at his house, but as his health deteriorated, he had no choice.

One Sunday afternoon, a loud knocking put fear in his children as their mother rose to open the door. Two men dressed in dark suits came into the sitting room. One was very tall and thin, and the other was short and fat with dark circles under his eyes. His clothes were one size too small, and Joey thought he looked like a stuffed sausage. "Too much pasta," he said under his breath.

They spoke in low whispers as Joey strained to hear what they were saying.

Joseph abruptly turned to his wife. "Take your children to the park." That was the code for her to leave him alone in the house. Too much knowledge was a liability and he had to protect his family. It was decided a long time before that he didn't want his sons following in his footsteps. He rationalized the misdeeds as a way to give his children a better life. He wanted them to be law-abiding citizens, away from the blood, anger and cruelty of the underground that had sucked him down. Joey had other ideas. He wanted to be just like his father. He watched and listened even though he knew he shouldn't.

Joey was at home when three men showed up at the door asking for his father. His mother was shopping with his sister and his brothers were out trying to scam money from people by selling cheap goods. "Take off," his father instructed him as he shoved him out the door. Joey found himself in front of the house with no coat. It was cold, and winter sleet hit the ground, making it difficult to walk on the sidewalk. He went back and hid in the hall with his ear pressed up against the door. Muffled voices escaped through the cracks, but Joey could not make out what they were saying. All of a sudden, the door opened and Joey spilled onto his kitchen floor. The three men laughed, holding their sides from the humor in it all, but Joey's father did not share in their joy. His face was stone-still as he said his goodbyes and closed the door.

"I thought I told you to leave," he said in a deadly voice. Joey had never heard his father take that tone with him and stepped back in surprise. Then he stopped and stood his ground. Something inside told him it was his chance to express his ambitions.

"I want to work with you, Pop." The words came out of his mouth before his brain could rationalize what he was saying.

Time stood still. His father stood in front of him with a strange look. For a moment, Joey thought it was a look of pride.

"I could collect your bets and go to the track for you. I could deliver messages in half the time it takes for you to walk down the street. I could be your right hand man and make your life easier."

Joey stood stunned as the back of his father's hand hit his face.

"No! No son of mine will be in this business," his father screamed, his eyes protruding from his head. "This is a dirty business. You get a real job."

Joseph ignored the situation and continued to fervently protect his family from his activities. He had good reason. If he sponsored his son, it would fall on him to take responsibility for any mistakes. He also knew that if his son were killed, he would surely lose the others. If you shoot one brother, you must shoot them all or face the vengeance of blood. Joey never mentioned it again, but he still yearned to feel the power and wanted people to look up to him as they did his father.

Joseph knew that his son wanted to follow in his footsteps. He worried that soon he would have no control. It was evident that his son did not intend to finish school and he needed a skill. Joseph approached his youngest son.

"I want you to learn a trade," he demanded. "I know a man who owns a wood shop close by. He owes me a favor and has agreed to take you on as an apprentice. Carpentry is a good profession and you will never go hungry if you learn how to build things."

"I don't want to," Joey insisted. "I would rather work on cars."

"Why do you want to have black grease under your fingernails?"

"I don't mind."

"Well, you learn this and then choose what you want to do."

"Do I have to, Pop?"

"Yeah, you have to! I don't want you to end up like your no-good brothers."

Nervously, Joey walked down the street with his father to the local carpenter, who had agreed to teach him a trade. He didn't want to work with wood, but he wanted to please his father. When Joseph left, the old man gave the young boy a hammer and led him to a back room stacked to the ceiling with piles of wood.

"Take each piece of wood and hammer out the nails," the old man instructed. "Then straighten each nail on this block of concrete and put them in each cigar box according to size."

Joey stared at the mountain of wood, and then he looked at the heavy hammer in his smooth, clean hands. Impatiently, the old man grabbed the hammer from him and demonstrated. "See? Like this." Then he was gone.

Trying not to hit his fingers on the block, Joey spent the whole day pounding nails. At the end of the day, Joseph came by to pick up his son. Dropping the hammer, Joey ran out to him, blinking in the sunlight.

"Please, Pop, don't make me come back here," he cried as they walked back home. Joseph listened to his son's complaints and remained silent as he thought of a solution.

"Let's give it one more day. I'm sure tomorrow will be different."

Joey stared down at the sidewalk as they walked home. He thought for sure his father was going to save him from the laborious task.

"Okay, I'll give it another try."

The next day, Joey walked to the carpenter's shop with his father, hoping he would say something to the old man. When he left, the man gave Joey the hammer and pointed to the wood.

"You know what to do," the man smiled, and then left.

Sick with despair, Joey was once more alone with the mountain, unaware of his father's plan. When the carpenter thought he was gone, Joseph sneaked back into the shop. When he saw his son laboring over the enormous stack of lumber, his blood began to boil. He ran at the carpenter, knocking the screwdriver in his hand clear across the room.

"You told me you needed an apprentice, but all you really wanted was free labor. I trusted you with my son and you betrayed me."

As Joseph left with his son, he turned to the old carpenter. "You haven't heard the last from me."

A few weeks later, Joey and his brothers passed the shop on their way to the train station. It was boarded up with a large "Closed" sign hanging on front door. No one ever discussed what happen to the old man and his shop, but Joey could not help smiling whenever he passed it. A twinge of guilt stirred inside him, knowing he might have been the cause of the old man's fate, but it was not as strong as the power he felt as his childhood innocence slipped away.

The Falcon

The falcon sits perched high, not in flight
Hoping to hear a kind word in the night

Beautiful falcon who once felt great pride
Dreams of soaring and descending with great glide

Long gone the speed and cunning in flight
This great bird knew in darkness of night

The falcon glories no more in feast
Time has no mercy for man nor beast

Though he may be large or small
Knowing of his inevitable fall

Upon this living thing remains a heart so bold
A welcome spring where time has taken hold

For now the falcon has lost his flight
Silently waiting for a kind word at night

— Gemini Joe

Chapter Seven

Hanging out under the corner streetlight, Joey and his friends stood smoking their cigarettes.

"I can't play pool tonight," Tony told his friends. I have a date."

"We told you to stay away from that girl," Jimmy lectured to his friend.

"You better watch out for her old man," Joey added.

"Her father doesn't scare me," Tony said with a smirk, exhaling the smoke from his cigarette. "He's nothing but an old, washed up mobster. Besides, we're in love, Annemarie and me. I'm meeting her at the movies in an hour."

"You're crazy, man. You're going to be swimmin' with the fishes if you don't watch it," Jimmy warned over his shoulder as he and Joey left for the pool hall.

Pool was Joey's game, and he was ruthless about keeping his title as a shark. It was easy money for him, but the look of dread from his competitors when he walked through the door bothered him. He wanted to win, but he also wanted them to like him. He couldn't have both. He settled on holding onto his rank. A cigarette hanging from his mouth, he skillfully took his shots, acting surprised when the ball hit its target and spun around the hole before it disappeared.

"I'm going to make some money tonight," Joey announced as they walked into the smoke-filled parlor.

Jimmy paid for the table as Joey began to eye the stick case, looking for his favorite lucky pool stick. He grabbed it and began to head toward a table. "Hey, that's mine," he heard a voice say. Before Joey turned to see the guy, he could smell the motorcycle grease that emitted from his body. "You must be new here," Joey snarled. "Everyone knows this is my stick."

The old biker stood firm. "Fuck you," he said. Joey could see his body tense up and his fist tightening, but he was not about to back down from this tough-guy. Jimmy walked up beside his friend, just in time to deter a fight.

"I got us a table. What's up?"

Joey reluctantly backed away from his potential aggressor. He really didn't want to fight and was relieved that the guy turned to walk away. The greaser smirked and joined his two friends at the bar.

"Let's make this look good," Joey whispered. "Rack 'em up, Jim, I'm gonna cream you," he yelled loud enough for the trio of men drinking at the bar to hear.

"In your dreams," Jimmy responded as he broke. He shot the first ball into the side pocket, keeping control over the table until he was ready to let Joey have a shot. They continued the game, loudly declaring their victories and defeats. Joey's luck ran out as Jimmy took over the table. Joey felt the eyes of the men at the bar on his back and knew he was about to be challenged.

"Hey, kid, do you want to have a game?" one of the men asked.

"I don't know," Joey said.

"Oh, come on. I'll even let your break."

Joey pretended to think for a moment. "Sure, why not?" he said as he racked up the balls.

"I'm Rick, and those are my friends Ted and James." Rick held out his hand.

"I'm Joey and that's Jimmy," Joey replied as he shook Rick's hand.

Joey chalked his cue and took the shot. The balls flew in different directions, but none sunk. Joey lost five dollars on the first game, and tried to look nervous.

"Let's go again," Rick insisted.

"I want to play him next," James yelled, jumping off his bar stool.

When Joey lost twenty dollars, he pretended to panic. "I'm losing all my money," Joey said as he counted the bills in his wallet. Ted noticed a couple of twenties before Joey put the wallet in his back pocket. Jimmy stood along the wall, puffing on a cigarette and trying not to laugh.

"Double or nothing," Ted shouted. "We'll give you a chance to win your money back."

"I don't think I should," Joey said, stepping away from the table.

"Come on, boy!" Rick added. "Don't you feel lucky?"

Joey looked over to Jimmy. "Should I play it for double or nothing?"

"What are you crazy? Do you want to lose everything?"

"You could win," Rick tempted.

"Well, okay," Joey smiled, and proceeded to wipe them out. They old bikers were not happy, but before they could realize it was a scam, Joey and Jimmy gathered their belongings and said that they had to get home. They walked out of the pool hall, grinning from ear to ear, and hoping that they wouldn't be jumped from behind. Safely back at their own street corner, they divided their spoils under the lamppost. "Wow, I really killed 'em tonight, didn't I, Jim?" Joey boasted.

"Yeah, but you're lucky you didn't get your ass kicked."

"Yeah, you might be right. What do you want to do now?"

"I think I'm gonna head on home. Are you coming?"

"No, I'm gonna wait for Tony."

"I'll see you tomorrow," Jimmy said before he disappeared into the shadows of the dark, empty street. Joey stood under the lamppost smoking a cigarette and looking up at the crescent moon in the sky. He strained to see the stars, but they hid behind the clouds that threatened to bring rain. After an hour, he began to wonder if his friend was distracted by his girlfriend and forgot about him.

When Tony finally showed up, Joey was halfway finished with the flask of vodka he had hidden in his pocket.

"Hey, give me a swig," Tony said as he grabbed the flask.

Joey laughed as his friend drank, glancing to make sure no cops were around. He hated them because they knew where he lived. They amused themselves by telling Tony's father about his misdeeds, knowing that his old man would whip him. His father did not want to draw attention to his business dealings, and the presence of the police every other night deterred his clients, who feared getting pinched. "How many times do I have to tell you to keep them cops out of my house?" Tony's father screamed.

Just as they were ready to call it a night, they noticed a car creeping down the street. Suddenly it stopped and five guys jumped out. Sensing danger, Tony and Joey took a defensive stance as the thugs surrounded them. "Which one of you is Tony?"

"I'm Tony. What's it to you?"

"You need to come with us. Someone wants a word with you."

Tony could see the gun in his pocket and swallowed hard.

"Where are you taking him?" Joey asked.

"Pennsylvania!"

Tony began to sweat. Everyone knew the empty lots on Pennsylvania Avenue were used for justice and revenge. "Can my friend come too?" Tony's eyes pleaded for Joey to stay with him.

The men looked at each other and laughed. "Sure, suit yourself."

Joey did not want to go but he couldn't let his friend get into the car without him. He wouldn't have been able to live with himself if he turned his back and something bad happened. They drove in silence until they arrived at the dark and foreboding road that everyone avoided, including the police.

When the door opened, they saw an old man waiting. "Is this the piece of shit that won't stay away from my daughter? Get out here, you scumbag!"

Joey was helpless as they dragged his friend from the car. The man watched with satisfaction as his five goons took turns beating Tony. "Not in the face," he warned. "Kick him in the back, kick him in the legs, but don't leave any marks on his face. You like my daughter, huh. I told you to stay away from her."

"I'll stay away," Tony cried. "I promise."

His pleas fell on deaf ears as they punched him in the stomach. The vodka shot out from his mouth like a fountain, followed by the popcorn he and Annemarie ate at the movies.

When the thugs left, Joey did his best to clean up his friend, and together they walked home in silence.

* * * * * *

"Joey, what are you studying?" Dom asked, and then grabbed the manual out of his brother's hands.

"Don't call me Joey. My name is Joe. And if you must know, I am studying for my driver's license."

"What? Why are you doing that?"

"Because I can!"

"Why can't you take the train like the rest of us?"

"I'm going to drive."

"Did you hear that Franc? Joey thinks he is going to get a driver's license," Dom yelled as he grabbed the book out of his brother's hands."

"My name is Joe!" he hollered and lunged toward his brother to retrieve his book.

"You don't even have a car," Franc chimed in, trying to discourage him.

"I'm going to have my license by summer," Joey boasted to his brothers.

"I'll believe it when I see it," Dom laughed.

Joe refused to let his brohers stop him and whenever they were not around, he studied the small yellow manual he'd picked up at the Department of Transportation.

A few weeks later at the dinner table, Joe sat with a permanent smile on his face. "What's wrong with you?" Franc asked. Everyone stopped eating to look at Joe. When all eyes gazed his way, he waved his certificate in the air.

"I passed," he told them. "I passed my driver's test."

They all took turns looking at the official paper allowing him to drive. Joe caught a hint of green in his brother's brown eyes and felt satisfied that he was the first to drive.

"What good is it?" Dom declared. "You have no car!"

He was right, but Joe had a plan. Joe loved cars and he was good at fixing them. Working as an apprentice at a local mechanic shop, he learned quickly.

"Hey, Joe, you're mechanically inclined!" The head mechanic praised.

"Watch out for those springs," the head mechanic warned. "If it snaps, it will take your head off."

Joe didn't care about the danger. He was making money and saving every dime. His father noticed how hard he was working. "I'm going to buy you a car," he promised Joe. "It may need some work, but you could fix it up."

The day Joe took ownership of an old, broken-down Ford was the happiest day of his life. He put his head under the hood and no one saw him for weeks. Jumping from under the hood to the driver's seat, he cranked the engine. Nothing! But soon the sound of the motor had everyone running outside to see. Joe sat behind the wheel, smiling and beating his fists on the dashboard with joy.

Gemini Joe

Joe became the designated driver for all his friends, and sometimes his brothers. By night, they cruised up and down the busy streets looking for girls. Joe spent most of his time fixing the old jalopy. He was able to fix everything except for the windshield wipers, which jammed up and froze in place. They were a problem during rain and snowstorms. When the weather made it necessary, Joe's friends would hang their heads out the windows and tell him which way to go as he blindly steered the car. The little group didn't have much money for gas, but resourceful Joe knew a trick. By lowering the nozzle in the right way, he was able to get a pint of gas from the pumps. It was just enough to get them around until they found another station.

Joe began working as a grease monkey, changing oil, filters and lubricating the engine. He was learning fast and he felt proud of himself. Soon he knew enough to look for a paying job. He was hired by Condon Motors in Brooklyn where he learned to work on brakes and clutches. When word came down that there was going to be a strike at Condon Motors, Joe worried that he might lose his job. If the workers held out for more money, Joe knew that he wouldn't be able to cross the picket line. He did not want to be out of money, so he applied for a job at Carol Motors six blocks away. They were impressed by his credentials and hired him on the spot. Joe was put on a time schedule. They gave him a car and a card to punch into a clock. Each mechanic was responsible for the repair time, ensuring they did not take too long or cheat the customers.

The owner of Carol Motors had a very spoiled daughter. Her father gave her a new car every year. Every week, she came into the shop and complained that she heard a squeaky noise coming from the car. No one could find the source of the noise.

"Let's give Joe a shot at it," one of the guys said in a mocking tone.

Joe took the car out for a test drive. Before long he returned, and without saying a word he put it up on the lift and began to work. The young lady came to pick up her car and drove off. Joe was working on another car when he was called to the office.

"Joe, you made my daughter very happy. No one else could fix her car. You are a heck of a mechanic. I'm giving you a raise." With an extra five dollars per week, Joe was able to save enough to buy a Chevy. It did not have mechanical problems and the windshield wipers actually worked.

* * * * * *

Trouble was around every corner as Joe and his friends took to the road.

"We need some liquor," Jimmy said as he jumped into the back seat and hung over into the front. In front of the liquor store, an older man was leaning against the wall smoking a cigarette.

"Hey, could you buy us a bottle," Joe yelled out to him.

"What's in it for me?" he asked.

"Well, we could share it with you," Tony offered.

Jimmy gave his friend a look, but it was too late. They parked the car and walked over to the man, who took their money and disappeared into the store. When he finally came out, they slid along the narrow alleyway on the side of the building. The man unscrewed the cap and put the brown-paper-bag-covered bottle up to his lips. They waited. The bottle did not come back down.

"Hey, slow down, don't drink it all," they said.

"Shut up, kid. I'll stop when I'm done."

Usually Dom bought them liquor, but he was busy with his new girlfriend, Tori. They could not rely on him and occasionally had to trust someone else. Sometimes they misjudged and asked the wrong person to buy for them, but it was all part of the risk.

Dom followed his youngest brother and applied for his driver's license, too. He did not have a car like Joe and had to walk with his date. He would wait for Joe to come home from work and jumped up when he heard the door open, hoping it was his brother.

"Joe, I'm so glad to see you," Dom said staring at the car keys, which Joe twirled around his finger, imitating Franc.

"I have a date with Tori tonight and I was wondering if you would do me a big favor—lend me your car." Before Joe could respond, he grabbed him by the shoulders, one eye pleading while the glass eye stared off in the opposite direction. "Please," he begged.

Joe lent him the car, thinking it would be a one-time thing, but found him handing over the keys more often than he liked. After a while, he couldn't get his car back.

"Dom, you can't keep taking my car," Joe tried to reason. He did not want to make his brother mad. "You never put gas in the car and you always bring it back empty."

"You have more money than me," Dom snapped.

Joe felt a fight coming on and backed off, but their father heard everything from the other room. He stormed into the kitchen and began to yell at Dom.

"Go get a job and buy your own car," he commanded.

"Stay out of it, old man," Dom screamed as they came uncomfortably close.

"Don't fight," Joe begged, trying to get between them before they came to blows. "It's all right. Dom can borrow the car."

Dom grabbed the keys and ran out the door.

"Don't forget to put gas in it," Joe said, trying to sound authoritative.

"Spineless wimp!" his father remarked under his breath. Joe knew that he lost his car but he refused to fight.

Florence felt sorry for her youngest son. "You're such a good boy, Joe. I know about someone who is selling a better car. Let's go check it out." Together they walked to the bank, where Florence withdrew enough money to buy the car.

When Dom came home from his date, he saw the car in front of the house. "Wow!" he said. "That car is great."

Joe tried not to smile. He had a better car now, thanks to his mother.

Dom must have impressed Tori, because they quickly married and she moved into the house. Franc was not happy to move out of their room and down to the basement, but he had no choice. The large house was still too small for the family to be in close quarters.

* * * * * *

Joe and his friends sought shelter from the hot summer sun under the boardwalk at Coney Island every day. But at night, it was time for cruising the neon-lit thoroughfare. Sandwiched in the back seat, Joe's friends never complained when they had a girl on their lap. When Joe was behind the wheel with the radio blasting and a pretty girl in the passenger seat, Joe felt like the king of the world and the prestige went to his head.

Joe was never at Sunday morning mass, but every Sunday night he attended the church dance. He could feel Father Murphy's eyes on him all night, because Joe and his crowd had a bad reputation.

Father Murphy was a small man with sandy red hair and a mustache. His high-collared black suit looked like it was strangling him and gave him a strained look. He presided over the music and kept a watchful eye on the dancers. "Not so close," he warned, making sure things didn't get out of hand. He had an uneasy feeling when Joe walked through the door. Joe was older than most of the others and had a reputation as a bad influence.

Joe's confidence gave him an air of excitement, and he attracted the girls who could not resist playing with fire. His good looks and finesse on the dance floor held all eyes as he spun his partners and stole everyone's attention with his moves. A hidden flask was passed around among his friends, and they each took a swig as they swirled their girls around the dance floor.

Joe saw Jean across the dance floor. She had just finished singing a song on stage and everyone gathered around with praise. Intrigued by her outgoing personality, Joe kept track of her all night. He noticed that she was staring at him too, but he avoided eye contact. When he saw Jean on the arm of her date, Joe began to feel jealous. He stepped up his dance moves, checking to see if she was watching. Joe was determined—Jean was going to be on his arm at the end of the night. He took every opportunity to talk to her.

"How old are you?"

"I'm eighteen," Jean lied. She was only sixteen.

"I have a new car. Would you let me take you home tonight?"

"I'm here with my boyfriend."

"He could come too, I guess."

Jean excitedly approached her boyfriend, Dominick. "Joe offered to give us a ride home in his car."

"No thanks, I'd rather walk."

"Don't be like that. Joe is a nice guy, and did you see his car?"

"I don't care. We're walking."

"No, you're walking. I'm going home with Joe."

Dominick noticed the smug look on Joe's face. Dominick loved Jean, but he didn't want to fight.

"Make sure she gets home safe," he instructed Joe.

"Of course," Joe said as he took Jean's arm and walked out the door.

* * * * * *

Jean was the youngest of four sisters. Her curly brown hair escaped in wisps from her hair clip and framed her copper-hued eyes. Perfectly shaped ruby red lips balanced her heart-shaped face. She was born with confidence. A fighter, she rarely let anyone push her or her family around. "I'll deck you," Jean warned the girls at the schoolyard. "You lay one hand on my sister Lucia and you'll wish you were never born." Rarely did she have to prove herself as the other girls backed down and let her have her way.

Jean and Lucia were inseparable by day, and whispered their secrets to each other in the bed they shared at night. Lucia was at the church dance the night Jean met Joe.

"Wasn't he dreamy," Jean cooed to her sister.

"He was good looking, that's for sure, but he seems very pushy."

"Oh, he's just a little conceited. He has charisma."

"I don't know," Lucia cautioned. "I think there is something strange about him. He drinks too much and he seems possessive."

The next Friday, Jean's father, Giuseppe Celestina, opened the front door to find Joe on the other side. Joe was holding a bouquet of flowers, trying to impress Mr. Celestina with his manners, but something did not seem right about Joe.

"Where is your family from?" Giuseppe asked.

"They're from America," Joe answered, even though he knew exactly what Jean's father meant.

"Yes, but where in Italy are they from?"

"My dad's family is from Naples, and my mom's family is from Tuscany."

Giuseppe clicked his tongue. He was from a small fishing village called Scicca in Sicily. He always found that Italians in the north were dishonest and could not be trusted.

"Make sure you bring my daughter home by ten o'clock."

"Don't worry, I'll get her home safe," Joe promised.

Giuseppe sat up, waiting for his daughter to come home. With four daughters, he had experience with male callers. Sitting in the chair, his mind wandered to other nights spent waiting for his daughters. Shy and timid Marie was the oldest. Then there was Phyllis, tough and cynical. His third daughter was Lucia, who was the peacemaker and very protective of her younger sister Jean. Jean was his baby and she inherited his talent for song. Giuseppe sang at weddings and family occasions, but was too busy to pursue a singing career. Jean promised that she would become a famous singer and make him proud.

From the minute he arrived in America as a boy of fifteen, Guiseppe worked hard. He wanted to be an American and signed up for the Army at seventeen. He married Anna a few years after he returned from the service. He knew that he would marry her when he first saw her skipping rope in the courtyard in front of her apartment building. Her long, blonde hair flowed down past her shoulders, and he feel in love instantly.

"I'm going to marry that girl someday," he told his friend.

"I think that she is too young for you," his friend replied.

Giuseppe made it a point to return often until he was considered a good family friend. When Anna turned eighteen, he decided to make his move, but was heartbroken to discover that Anna already had a boyfriend. He'd waited too long.

Anna was engaged to a young man named Alfred, and they were deeply in love. But Alfred's mother was not convinced that she was right for her son.

"I want you to come and clean my house next Saturday, Anna. Then I will know if you are a good housekeeper," her future mother-in-law requested.

Anna did not want to be tested like this, but she loved Alfred. She knew that her mother would not allow her to clean someone else's house, so she kept it a secret. When Anna returned home the next Saturday afternoon, her beautiful hands were raw from the abrasive cleaners and constant soaking in water.

"What happened to you?" her mother asked. "Why are your hands so red?"

When Anna admitted where she had been all day, her mother became very angry. Anna had never seen her mother this mad and feared the worst.

"What kind of man is this that would degrade his future wife? You will not marry into this family. I forbid it."

Anna cried, but knew her mother was right. It was a horrible ordeal. Even in her own house, she was not subjected to such harsh treatment. Alfred did nothing to protect her. Being the dutiful daughter, she obeyed her mother and cried into her pillow every night until the pain subsided. Giuseppe took the opportunity to console her. She did not love him like she loved Alfred, but he was a good man and her family loved him.

Finally, Giuseppe heard the car pull up. He heard Jean slip quietly into the house. She did not notice her father sitting in the dark and jumped when she heard his voice.

"Who is this Joe?" her father asked.

"He's a boy I meet at the church dance," Jean replied.

"What happened to Dominick?"

"Dominick? He is mad at me and I don't care. Anyway, he's boring."

"I suppose Joe isn't boring?"

"Oh, Pop, Joe is so nice. He treats me special and he is very protective. I know you will like him once you get to know him."

Something was off with Joe, but Mr. Celestina could not put his finger on it. He seemed to be hiding something about himself, but he couldn't convince his daughter, so he held back his words, hoping she would lose interest in him.

Jean continued dating Joe. She wondered why Dominick never attempted to get her back, but Joe kept her busy. Once he brought her home to meet his family, they did not go on dates. Instead, they spent most evenings watching his fish swim in the tanks along the wall in Joe's small room. Jean was uncomfortable when she heard his family fighting in the next room.

"I have to go home now," she told Joe, who had been drinking heavily all night.

Joe stood in front of his bedroom door. "Don't go yet," he demanded.

"I have to go. My father is waiting up for me."

"You need to listen to me, not your father," Joe slurred.

"I have to go!" Jean tried to push Joe out of her way.

"If I drop something on the floor, you have to pick it up," Joe ordered her.

"No, I don't," Jean replied.

"Yes, you do," Joe insisted, and threw a book down in the middle of the room.

Jean tried again to push him away from the door.

"You can leave after you pick that up," Joe said as he blocked her way.

Feeling trapped, Jean began to panic. Tears spilled down her face as she yelled, "Let me out!"

Joe's mother knocked on the door.

"What's going on in there!" she yelled. "Open this door right now, Joe."

No sooner than the door opened, Jean rushed past his mother and flew down the stairs. She ran all the way home and did not look back. Out of breath, she ran past her father and shut herself in her room.

Joe realized he had gone over the line when he became sober. He could not believe he was capable of acting like that. Just like his father. He always swore that he would not treat his girl the way his father treated his mother.

"I'm so sorry," Joe told Jean on the phone. "My mother is mad at me and wants you to come back so I can apologize in front of her. I think I just drank too much. It will never happen again, I promise."

Jean reluctantly accepted his apology, but began to think something was odd about Joe. Joe's mother wasn't feeling well, but insisted on having Jean at the Sunday dinner table. Sitting around the table with Joe's family, Jean felt a little out of place. Everyone was talking at once and their voices rose when they disagreed with each other. Jean sat quietly, moving the fork around her plate. She could tell that Joe's mother was the peacemaker and felt sorry for her. Jean sensed that dealing with the forceful men in her family was exhausting. They did not seem to care that she was frail and tired. But Florence cooked a wonderful meal and tried to make Jean feel comfortable at her home.

The Fear of Death

One of the fears of living is death
Yet no one knows for sure

These are many fears in life itself
Could then death be something to fear

We know for sure our lives have many fears,
Sadness, sickness, loneliness and much more

From the beginning like death darkness was also feared
And man favored the light of day

God made man for living and death
just as he made light and darkness

— Gemini Joe

Chapter Eight

Florence never questioned the source of the family finances. She knew better than to ask her husband too many questions, especially ones she might not want to hear the answers to. She kept busy running the household, cooking, shopping, cleaning and taking care of her four children. There was no reason for her to concern herself with money. That is, until Joseph gave her the news that he lost the house on a bad bet. Distraught and furious with her husband, she ran into her bedroom, locking the door behind her. The money she had been hiding in the back of her drawer now had a use as she shoved it into her purse and ran out of the house. "Watch your brother," she told Dolly over her shoulder as she slammed the door shut. Florence paid off her husband's debt and retrieved the deed to the house, but she insisted that it be in her name. "I will not live with the fear of losing my home!" she screamed.

Joseph contained his anger. He was glad to have the house back, but he wasn't happy with the liberties his wife took. Still, he knew that she wouldn't drop it and decided to give in this one time. "All right," he begrudgingly agreed, and took his name off the property, eliminating any future risk of losing it. Not taking any chances, she had a will drawn up, stating that in the unlikely event of her demise, her children would be the beneficiaries. This made Florence feel more secure. She knew that her husband's vices had a negative effect on the family. Florence then returned to pretending that everything was the way it should be, and again she turned a blind eye to her husband's activities.

Florence was only forty-five years old, but some days she felt very tired. Dressed for work and ready to start the day, she couldn't muster the energy to leave the house. "I don't feel well," she would say, stopping at the door. "I don't think I'll be going to work today."

Years of working took its toll on Florence, and sometimes she worried about the effects of the blue dye from her factory days. She tried her best to hide it, but she knew that something was wrong. But if her family noticed that she was becoming weaker, no one voiced concern for fear of what might happen. Her fatigue grew as she lost weight, and she seemed to disappear before their eyes. Countless trips to the doctor did not give any reasons for her ill health. She stopped complaining and kept her suffering to herself. As her health deteriorated, she became homebound. Extensive tests resulted in the discovery of a small tumor. She heard her husband whispering with the doctor but she could not get past the silent wall he put up.

"You just have a growth that needs to come out. It will be fine," he assured her. But she knew that her husband was holding back information about her illness.

After several operations, she was relieved to be rid of the cancer, but in a few months, she relapsed. It was getting harder for Florence to keep up the pace at the luncheonette.

"Vitamins," Joseph told his wife on the drive home from the doctor. "That's what you need."

No one in the family wanted to acknowledge the fatal prognosis. Denial drove them to keep it an unspoken truth. Florence was exhausted. Clearly, she could no longer spend hours on her feet cooking. When Joseph's brother, Pat, offered to take over at the luncheonette, it was one less thing to worry about.

Joseph knew his wife didn't have long to live. He began to worry about the house. If anything happened, he would have no control. He gathered his children together. "Come alone," he instructed, insisting that it was a family matter and not for outsiders. "Mom is having surgery next week. She is going to be fine," he quickly added. "But just in case this next surgery doesn't go well, I need you to sign this paperwork."

"This is Mom's will," Dolly said as she passed it along for Joe to read.

"I need you all to sign the house back to me in case something goes wrong. Your mom didn't know she was going to get sick when she had it written up."

Franc and Dom stared at each other across the kitchen table. They didn't want to sign the house back to him, but how could they refuse? "Mom's not going to die!" Dom angrily told his father.

"Of course not," Joseph assured them. "It's just a precaution."

After the operation, Florence seemed to regain her strength. That's what her family expected, and that's what she was determined to do.

"Get dressed, we're going out," Joseph told her in the morning. He piled the whole family into the car and drove to Lakewood, New Jersey.

"Where are we going?" Florence asked.

"It's a surprise," Joe smiled.

"Yeah, don't ask questions," Dom chimed in.

"I don't want to go," Franc whined. "I have a date with my fiancée, Mary."

"You're going. Shut up and get in the car."

"They're squishing me," Joe complained.

As the car drove over the bridge out of New York, Joseph's children pinched and pushed each other. "Settle down, right now!" Joseph warned them. "You're upsetting your mother."

They pulled off the exit and the city began to melt away.

"Hey, I don't see the buildings," Joe said as he looked out of the back window. Nothing but the road and the trees remained as they continued for another few miles. Just as the noise from the back seat came to a roar, the car pulled onto a dirt road.

"Close your eyes before we go any further," Joseph said to Florence.

"That's silly," she laughed. Franc reached behind his mother's seat and covered her eyes with his hands. "No peeking!" they all yelled. The children pushed and fought once again as their excitement grew. They bounced up and down as the tires hit potholes and the crackling sound of gravel almost drowned out their bickering. Then total silence. No one said a word as they stared at the large lake that loomed up in front of them.

"What's going on?" Florence asked, not used to the calm. One by one, they climbed out of the car. Franc and Florence were last because he still had his hands covering her eyes. "I'll keep them closed. I promise."

"Careful," Joseph cautioned his son. "Don't let her peek."

When they were all outside the vehicle, Joseph stood next to his wife. "Okay. Open your eyes."

"What is this? Where are we?"

"This is where we are building our new country house," Joseph announced proudly.

For the first time, the family stood together without fighting.

They excitedly made plans for the new home. Seeing her family so happy, Florence began to cry. "I love it," she repeated over and over. It was a magical day.

But when they arrived home, a draft notice was waiting for them. Florence's youngest son was going to war. "Don't worry, ma. I'll be fine," Joe said. But he was scared. He never liked to fight.

Every weekend they went back to the lake, delivering cement blocks and building materials for the log cabin they planned to build. Joseph knew it would never get finished in time, but it seemed to bring his family some amount of unity. He continued the deception.

* * * * * *

The family spent less and less time at the luncheonette, losing interest and relying on Uncle Pat to take care of it. Joseph wasn't surprised when his brother paid him a visit at the house one night.

"I want to take over the luncheonette. I want to buy it from you," he added before his brother could say no.

Joseph stared at his brother, who twitched nervously. He had neglected the business since his wife fell ill. Someone had to be in charge, and Pat needed a job.

Florence nodded her approval from across the room.

"All right," Joseph hesitantly said, "but I expect to be paid."

"Don't worry! I have so many ideas. We can't lose." Pat excitedly shook his brother's hand as he rushed out the door.

Joseph drove Florence to the doctor and stayed close by when she called for him. Without the luncheonette, he no longer had an excuse to leave the house and resented her for being a burden. He sometimes thought his wife was using her illness to keep him home. He felt that she was a weight around his neck.

Franc's fiancée, Mary, was tough as nails, with a mouth that could turn a sailor's face blue. She was a forceful woman, bossy and opinionated. She fit right in at the Fuccino household. She was at the house so much, no one was surprised when she came in with an engagement ring on her finger. After a small family wedding, Mary moved in permanently and took over. When Florence was too weak to cook, she jumped in and became the main cook, except for Sundays. Joseph insisted on cooking Sunday Sauce, because he thought Mary used too much fatty sausage. He preferred a leg of lamb and stood over his pot for hours to skim the excess grease. He enjoyed having control over Sunday dinner and insisted that the whole family sit around the table together.

"Uncle Pat changed the name of the luncheonette," Franc announced one Sunday dinner.

"He changed the menu, too," Dom added.

Dolly sat silently, but everyone knew something was eating at her. Finally she broke her silence. "You old bastard," she berated her father. "You should have kept it in the family. Tori and I could have run the place. We're good enough to cook for you, but not for the restaurant?"

"Be quiet, Dolly," Tori whispered, kicking her under the table.

"No! Everyone knows that Uncle Pat will run that place into the ground."

"You're not too old for me to smack you," Joseph warned his daughter. Dolly's husband remained quiet. He knew better than to get in the middle of a Fuccino fight.

"You just try to hit me," Dolly yelled and stood up in a defensive stance.

Florence awoke to the commotion and painfully made her way toward the kitchen. She was the only one who could soothe her volatile family.

"Mama, what are you doing up?" Joe asked as he jumped up to steady her wobbling frame. She was too weak to stand on her own but refused to leave them fighting like animals. Joe felt bad. His mother was sweet but she had no backbone. The rest of his family was loud, abrasive and mean, but Joe was powerless to help. He took after his mother, avoiding confrontation with his father and brothers.

"Get back to bed now, we'll be quiet," Tori promised.

The rest of the meal went down in lumps as the family hurried to finish and get away from each other. Dolly had a good point and Joseph knew it, but the deal was done and he was not about to admit he was wrong. But before Joseph saw a penny of the loan, the luncheonette closed. Pat made too many changes. People stopped coming. It just wasn't the same.

* * * * * *

Florence lost her fight with cancer in December of 1949. Every time they cut out a tumor, it grew back, bigger and meaner, invading her small body until her organs began to shut down one by one. The family was not prepared for her death. Joe was only twenty years old when he woke to the news of his mother's death.

"Joe, wake up!" Mary yelled as she banged on his bedroom door. The pounding of her fists felt like a sledgehammer to his head. He had one of the worst hangovers he ever experienced and wanted to roll over and go back to sleep. But the urgency in her voice caused him to bolt out of bed.

"What? What is it?"

"Get up! Your mother's dead!"

Joe stood frozen with his hand on the doorknob. "I must be having a nightmare," he thought. "Maybe if I go back to bed, I will wake up later and…"

"Did you hear me, Joe? Your mother is dead!"

Joe ran into his parents' room to see his father crying in the corner chair. He looked over to the bed where she lay. Her mouth was open and her eyes rolled back inside her head. Joe stared in disbelief as the aura of death surrounded him. Cancer had taken over her petite body, but the secret of her disease remained with the doctor and his father. She had been sick for a long time. Everyone took it for granted that she would fight the tumors. She was the most beautiful person in Joe's life, and even though he was not a child any longer, the loss of his mother devastated him. Her sudden death sent shockwaves throughout the family.

"Pop, why didn't you tell us?" his brothers cried.

"I wanted her to think she could get well. I wanted to give her hope. You would have acted different and roused her suspicion."

Dolly was weeping uncontrollably. Even through their grief, Joe's twin brothers were furious with their father. They had given their mother a lot of grief and they wished they had treated her better. Joe watched his grandmother sitting very quietly. Carmella stared at her oldest daughter's body, making no sound.

She is one strong lady, Joe thought as he drove Carmella home to prepare for the funeral. You're only allowed one mother, he thought.

Joe was crushed, and he used his pain to gain Jean's sympathy. "I'm so alone," he cried.

"You're not alone, Joe, you have me." Jean's heart went out to him. She promised to write to Joe everyday while he was in the service.

Shortly after Christmas, still mourning his mother's death, Joe left the house early in the morning. He felt for the dime in his pocket, given to him by the Army for his train fare to Fort Dix, New Jersey, for basic training. He did not fear war. He had just lost his mother and didn't care what happened to him. She was the thread that held the family together and once she was gone, they all began to unravel quickly.

Absence

If love could live in absence of times apart,
Time will show the quality of ones heart.
So like the fires that temper the steel
Soon time will tell if the love was real.

— *Gemini Joe*

Chapter Nine

After Florence's death, the rest of the family tried to co-exist in the big brick house. Like dogs circling before settling down to rest, they shuffled to find their space. Dolly lived on the main level with her husband, Tony, who lost his leg in the Second World War. The Japanese opened fire on his Navy ship, giving him his ticket home when a piece of scrap metal seared his leg.

Franc and Mary took the top floor apartment with their three daughters, while Joseph moved to the downstairs apartment at the back of the house. Dom, Tori, and their two daughters took the other downstairs apartment at the front of the house. Joe's small room, off the hall, remained empty until he came home on leave from the Army.

Downstairs, Joseph sat in his chair, sucking air from the tubes that provided oxygen while pumps sucked out the phlegm pooling in his lungs. He was unapproachable as he stared from across the room: his empty, dark, tormented eyes did not seem to reveal a soul and warned everyone to keep their distance.

When everyone was in their place, the fighting commenced. A spark ignited in one area of the house and quickly spread. Voices rose to the rooftop. Red-hot anger incited strings of profanity that echoed through the halls.

"You little bastards," Dolly yelled. The pictures on the living room walls bounced with the steady thump that was coming from the hall. "Quit it. Go outside with that ball," she yelled to her nieces. There were a few minutes of silence then the bouncing started once more as the ball hit the wall. "Stop it, I said, or I'm going to tell your mother."

"Go ahead. She told us we could play here," the oldest girl, Pamela, smugly told her aunt.

Dolly knew that her sister-in-law instructed them to stand their ground. "Mary, come and get your children," she screamed up the stairs. There was no response. She couldn't win this battle, and if she tried, it would only make matters worse. "Cathy, go out and play with your cousins," she told her daughter. "Get them to play something else."

The screams and cries outside woke the sleeping dragon. Mary tore down the stairs and ran outside. "What are you doing to my daughter, you little brat?" she accused Cathy.

"I didn't do anything. It was Pam. She was trying to get the ball away from Jenny."

"No, I wasn't," Pam smiled as she turned away from her mother. "Cathy is lying."

"Girls, get upstairs now. I don't want you playing with her anymore," Mary instructed.

Cathy stood alone on the sidewalk. If her two older sisters were home, it would not have been two against one.

The next time Dolly went to visit her father she made a special trip to his favorite bakery.

"I'll take two cannoli," overflowing with ricotta filling, "and two Napoleon," Bavarian cream layered between crisp puff pastry, "and two Pasticcotti," tarts filled with lemon custard. The baker lined them neatly and tied a red string around the box. Dolly never went empty handed when she visited her father, nor anyone else for that matter. It was just something that her mother taught her. The politeness did not go unnoticed by he father, whose eyes lit up when he saw the little white box.

"What did you bring me?" he asked, as excited as a small child.

Dolly waited until he was halfway through the pastries.

"Pop, you need to do something about Franc's kids. That son-of-a-bitchin' bastard, Mary, lets them do whatever they want. They make a mess and I constantly have to clean up after them." Dolly knew telling her father would cause trouble, but she needed to convince him that her brothers and their families could not be trusted.

"They live here and do nothing," she continued, depositing poison drops of doubt in her father's ear and giving him one more reason to fight with his sons.

Joseph sat in his chair thinking about his family. He felt his control slipping away along with his health. The more he thought about it, the angrier he became. Rage was brewing inside as he waited to hit the very next target that came through his door. He won the jackpot when the whole clan came to see him one Sunday afternoon.

"Get out of my house," Joseph yelled. "All of you!"

Dom's pregnant wife sat quietly at the kitchen table, listening to her husband and father-in-law fight. Unsure if she should stay or go, Tori looked to Franc for support.

"Stop it, Pop," Franc demanded.

"If you don't like it, then leave," Joseph barked, as he rose from his chair, willing his legs to hold him up. "You can't live here free. You need to pay rent."

"Please," Tori cried, as she held her swollen belly. "We will get the money. Tell him, Dom."

Dom refused to concede. "You don't need my money. You have plenty."

"I'll see you all fighting in the streets before you get my money," Joe's father screamed bitterly at his children.

Joe was only home for a week, on leave. He felt bad for his sister-in-law and feared that all the fighting might hurt her unborn baby. He hated the daily feuds and felt embarrassed that he was part of the family.

"Pop, don't yell. Dom will pay you the rent," Joe chimed in.

"You're all no good," Joseph snarled, "you and your brothers."

"He'll give you the money," Joe repeated, trying to sound convincing. But he knew better. Ever since Dom lost his eye, he used his handicap to manipulate his family.

Joe waited for his chance to escape out the side door. Like a volcano that erupts, it was best to stay clear from the path of his father's scourging anger. By the next day, the fighting subsided, but the tension hung in the air, lurking until the next battle.

Joseph seemed to enjoy the fights that accelerated to a feverish pitch. He faced off with his sons, trying to prove he was the master of the house. When he became tired from arguing, he returned to his chair, shaking his head with a look of disgust. The ground quaked with every step.

Joe's brothers seemed determined to suck up their inheritance even before their father was gone. Every few days, Joseph heard familiar words.

"Pop, could you lend me some money?"

Joe felt the tremors that indicated another eruption was on the horizon. He thought his family would kill each other before it was over, and he hated the confrontations. When his mom was alive, she was able to smooth things out, but now there was no one to prevent the verbal battering they inflicted on one another.

* * * * * *

Tori ran up the stairs to Mary's apartment and flung the door open. "Help me," she cried, barricading the door.

"What's wrong?" The words came out before Mary saw the knot on Tori's face. "What happened? Did Dom do this?" Both women jumped as heavy fists pounded the door.

"Get out here, you bitch," Dom slurred. "Get back downstairs where you belong."

"You're drunk. Go back downstairs and sleep it off," Mary yelled. "Tori is staying here tonight."

The door shook as Dom used his body as a battering ram. Mary's children, awakened by the noise, peeked out from their bedroom, terrified by their uncle's anger.

"Open this door—now!"

"Go back to your whore. Leave me alone," Tori cried.

Her words ignited a fuse, and his anger exploded from every pore. "When I get my hands on you, I'll kill you."

The two women knew this to be true, and held onto each other, waiting for the door to rip open. While Dom yelled and cursed, another voice joined him in the hall. Franc came home to find his twin brother with his hands bloodied from the beating he gave the front door. "She's a bitch and I'm going to kill her," Dom yelled.

"Forget about it! Come downstairs, let's talk," Franc consoled his brother. Dom often beat his wife in a drunken rage. His twin brother was different. Franc never raised his hand to Mary. He had a better temperament, or maybe he knew his wife could mop the floors with him. She was tough, but that was what he loved about her. Franc stayed with his brother until Dom passed out then went upstairs to let Tori know it was safe to go home. Tori quietly slipped into bed alongside her sleeping husband. He drank too much and didn't hide the women he saw on the side, but she loved him and was about to have his baby. If only she could keep her mouth shut, but it was not in her nature. She often said too much and suffered the consequences. "No good family!" she said out loud. "No good, from the father down to the sons."

* * * * * *

Joe was glad that he had his driver's license. The Army needed drivers, and he could drive Army vehicles and tanks. His mechanical attributes kept him safe and, assigned to the mechanical division, he used his ability to fix motors to his advantage, being promoted to sergeant of the motor pool within six months. Still, he hated the Army. He wanted to go home. Home to Jean, whom he imagined had forgotten about him as she laughed and danced with other guys. He was tempted to go AWOL, but he promised his mother when he was drafted he would not follow Franc, who was drafted into World War II in 1939. He could see his mother's face as he remembered that day.

Franc was home only one week when there was a knock on the door. Joe recalled how scared his mother was when she opened the door and saw two military police standing in front of her, rifles strapped to their shoulder. She thought they were going to shoot him.

"We've come for your son. He's gone AWOL. Is he here?"

"I'll see," she said as she closed the door and headed toward Franc's room.

Her body shook and tears welled up in her eyes. Gently, she shook Franc to wake him. "Franc, wake up," she whispered.

Franc sat up in bed. Dom also woke up.

"The police are here to pick you up," she cried.

Dom jumped up out of his bed. "I'll put your uniform on and go back with them," he told Franc. "By the time they realize they have the wrong man, you can get away."

"No," Franc smiled. "You're a good brother and I appreciate what you are willing to do for me, but I have to face it."

Dressed in his uniform, he hugged his sobbing mother.

"Please, Mom, don't cry. I'll be back soon."

Then he was gone. He spent the next two years in the stockade. No one spoke of it when he returned and he didn't offer.

Joe missed his mother, but he was glad she didn't have to kiss another son goodbye to the Army. She would have been proud of him, he was sure. No, he wouldn't go AWOL. He would serve his time with honor and courage.

Joe wrote to Jean every day, telling her he was depressed and lonely. She wrote back to him and tried to keep his spirits up. The words he wrote on paper revealed a different side of Joe. Not the tough, confident man that he showed the outside world, but a tender, sensitive man with deep feelings and a desire to be loved. Every night, Jean read some of his letters to her sisters.

One and Only

To my one and only love
God created you for me to love

He picked you out from all the rest
Because he knew, I loved you best

I once had a heart so brave and true
Now it's gone from me to you

If I go to heaven and your not there
I'll paint your face so you are near

Then the angels will know and see
Darling exactly what you mean to me

If your not there on judgment day
I'll know you've gone the other way

I'll give the angels back their wings,
Golden heirlooms and those things

Just to show my love is true
I'll go to hell to be with you

— Gemini Joe

"That's nice," Mary said. "He seems like a sensitive guy."
"Those are the ones you need to look out for," Phyllis warned.
"I'm glad you're happy, Jean," Lucia said as she hugged her sister.

Writing was easier than dating, and romantic feelings started to stir within Jean. The letters kept coming. Jean watched everyday for the mailman carrying his heavy pack of letters.

"Here he comes," Jean yelled and ran out of the house. Impatiently she waited while he fumbled to see if he had any mail for her. She stopped breathing for a second when she saw his hand reach out to her. Jean grabbed the letter and ran back home, flopping on her bed to read it in private. Her sisters came running in when they heard her excitement. Jean was jumping up and down on her bed. "He's coming home! Joe's coming home on leave."

Joe was miserable in the Army, but his station in Michigan was a relief from his combative family. Heartbroken by the death of his mother, he went to visit her grave his first day home on leave. When he could not find her name on the stone that marked the family plot, he went to the cemetery office in a fury and demanded to know why his mother was missing.

"No one came to order the engraving," the clerk told him.

"How much will it cost me?" Joe asked.

"Sixty-five dollars. I'll have it done by next week."

"But I am only on leave for a few more days," Joe told the clerk.

"I'll do it tomorrow, but it will cost you another ten," the clerk bargained.

Joe agreed and returned the next day with the money. He watched the engraver etch his mother's name into the stone.

"Cut it deeper than the other names," Joe instructed the engraver. He wanted to make sure his inconsiderate family noticed it.

Joe was satisfied with his vengeful request as he left the cemetery to confront his father.

"Why did you leave mom in an unmarked grave?" The words shot out as he burst into his father's room. Looking up from his paper, disdain for his son replaced his surprise. Joseph was not used to his youngest son challenging him and was not about to let him get away with it.

"What's the difference," he yelled. "It won't bring her back."

"Don't you care about your family?" Joe asked.

"Why should I? My family does nothing for me. My friends are more valuable than my family. Get out of here and leave me alone!"

Stunned by his father's words, Joe left with a heavy heart. He tried to make sense of his family as he stared out the window, leaving the city behind him. It was dog-eat-dog. No one in his family was sensitive to another's suffering. They seemed to take pleasure in it. Destroying people made his father feel good, and it didn't matter to him if they were blood relatives or not.

* * * * * *

During his times on leave, Joe stayed away from the house as much as possible. He knew his family members were at each other's throats and he did not want to get caught in the middle. Back at the house, the fighting among his family increased in velocity and pitch.

"Mommy, Uncle Franc's dogs pooped in the hall again."

"What? You go upstairs and tell them to clean it up, now," Dolly instructed her daughter.

"No one's home," she reported soon after.

Dolly's blood boiled as she put on a sweater and slipped into her shoes. She was so mad she knocked her daughter into the wall as she stormed out of the apartment and ran up the stairs.

"Open the door," she screamed. "Your dogs shit in the hall again." When there was no answer, she pounded on the door. "I know you're in there, you bitch."

"Beat it! It's snowing and I don't feel good," her sister-in-law growled from behind the door.

"You can't coop up two German Shepherds in a house. They need to do their business! If you think you're going to leave it for me to clean up, you have another thing coming."

"Goddamn it! I'll clean it when I'm ready, now get the fuck away from my door!" Mary's shill scream escaped from the crack of the door before it slammed shut.

Dolly ran back downstairs and rummaged through the closet for a shovel. Her daughter stood wide-eyed. She watched as her mother scooped up the dog shit and carefully carried it upstairs. Before long, the house echoed with Mary's screams.

"You fucker!" she yelled, scraping the bottom of her shoes. Dolly smiled as she finished cleaning the supper dishes.

* * * * * *

Each day ended in a shouting match between Joseph and one of his sons. Joseph was losing his ability to fight as he became weaker every day, but his rage simmered as he lost control over his house and found himself at his children's mercy.

Automated laundromats replaced door-to-door cleaning services, putting him out of business. Without the cover of the laundry service for his gambling activities, Joseph backed down and let the local gangs take over his turf. He turned his attention to his family, trying to get his sons to pay their share of the living expenses. Bitter words shot from his mouth, directed at whoever dared to walk through his door.

He was surprised to look up and see Franc.

"Hi, Pop! How are you feeling today?"

"Don't tell me that you give a shit!"

"Come on, Pop. Don't be that way!"

"What's this I hear about dogs? What makes you think you could bring two big German shepherd police dogs into my house?"

"There're not bothering anyone," Franc exclaimed defensively.

"Well, I hear different," Joseph fought to suck in air. "Dolly says they are dangerous and dirty. She also says that Mary lets them out into the hall. Dolly had to fight with her to pick up the shit!"

"Dolly over-exaggerates! When I came home, Mary was upset, and I had to hear about it."

"Well, I told Dolly she has my permission to lay down the law!"

"Tell your daughter to stop harassing my wife," Franc demanded as his father fought to catch his breath.

"Go to hell and take your family with you," Joseph spat at Franc as he reached for his ventilator, placing the tube into a hole in his throat. Although his health had deteriorated, he could not resist a good fight. "Don't come to me with your problems. Get out, all of you!" Joseph bellowed.

Dolly checked on Joseph during the day. At night, she passed the chore off to her brothers, Franc and Dom, who begrudgingly satisfied their father's needs.

"Who needs you?" Joseph sparred with his sons." If you don't want to help me, go away and don't come back."

"Why do we have to be stuck with him," Dom complained to his brother. "What about Joe? Call that little bastard. Get him over here."

Franc picked up the phone to call his younger brother. He didn't want to, but he didn't trust Dom, who was abrupt and combative.

"Hello, Joe. It's Franc. I need to talk to you about Pop."

"What now?" Joe moaned into the receiver.

"Joe, you do nothing to help take care of Pop. The burden is all on us."

"What do you want me to do?" Joe nervously asked.

"I don't know. Take him to the doctor," Franc suggested.

Joe let out his breath. This was something he could handle. The next afternoon, Joe held his father's arm and they took small steps toward the car. He tried to remain neutral as he endured his father's complaints about his older siblings. The doctor's office was two blocks away, but it felt like ten. Joe sighed with relief as his father disappeared into the treatment room. When he came out of the office, they walked in silence to the car. Joe wanted to lighten the mood. On the way home, instead of a right, he turned left.

"Where are we going?" Joseph demanded.

Joe ignored his father's anger.

"I want to go home. Take me home now!"

Joe pulled the car up in front of a luncheonette. Jumping out of the car before his father could protest, he yelled over his shoulder, "Sit tight, Pop, I'll be right back."

Joseph had no choice and sat growling to himself in the front seat. Finally he caught sight of his son holding an Italian ice in each hand, just like Joseph made when they owned their luncheonette. A rare smile crept across Joseph's face as his son handed him the ice.

While they enjoyed their Italian ices, Joe drove to LaGuardia airport. When he was small, his father drove him to the edge of the runway to watch the planes take off and land. Joe parked on the roadside so he and his father could finish their ices. They laughed at the sign on the fence: "Warning, Low-Flying Planes." The sign was amusing because this was the place they felt most safe. The outside world seemed to melt away under the thunder of the engines. On the drive home, they opened the windows to catch some air. As a child, Joe stuck his head out of the car window as his father drove. Now Joe was in the driver's seat and his father was the one with his head out the window.

When Joe dropped his father off at home, the good feelings they shared seemed to evaporate in the heat of the sun. "Just leave me here, I'll make it back by myself," Joseph barked.

"No, Pop, I'll help you," Joe pleaded, taking his father's arm and leading him into the house.

"My children are worthless," Joseph said as he pulled away from his son." I can't rely on any of you to take care of me. The only respect I get is from my friends."

"I don't see your friends here taking care of you," Joe snapped, angry at his father's lack of gratitude.

"My friends would spit in your face if they heard you," Joseph told his son with a sinister smile. "Just get me inside and leave. I've had enough of you for one day."

Return to the Woods

The parting from one you love hurts as memories linger
You long to look on the face of your love.
You desire to hear their voice or hold them in your now empty arms
To feel the warmth of their breath upon your neck
and bask in all their charms

Love can be a serpent
When bit, it hurts so much
You feel its venom waste you and hold you in its clutch
Pain of heart and stomach, a lack of desire to eat
The body is so tired yet doesn't welcome sleep.

A forever cloud surrounds you
your heart is worn and still
You feel that you will surely die
If the serpent has its will

Return to the woods where the serpent dwells
Seek him out, confront him
Soon you will know if the venom is poison
Or something you just fear within

Yes, return to the woods and relive what you were
When the answer has been answered
You can leave that woods and travel another road
With a newfound wisdom

— Gemini Joe

Chapter Ten

The Army whipped Joe into the best shape of his life. At the beach, strangers crowded around to watch him as he bench-pressed his friends, one at a time, over his head, his tan body glistening in the summer sun. A slender physique plumped up by massive muscles, Joe was somewhat of a ham and loved the attention he attracted as he showed off his strength. Popularity with the girls caused some resentment among his friends, but they maintained respect for Joe. No one wanted to provoke his famous family temper and become a casualty of his rage.

Jean hated the attention he craved from people around him. Joe knew it and used every opportunity to make her jealous with the girls.

"Marry me and you will have me all to yourself," he begged.

"Are you proposing?" Jean beamed. "I will have to talk to my family first."

"No! They will talk you out of it. Let's just go to the courthouse and elope."

"I can't do that to my mother! It will kill her."

"We'll talk to them together," Joe insisted.

Just as Jean expected, her father was upset.

"You're too young to get married," Giuseppe shouted.

"I'm almost eighteen," Jean reminded her father. "Mama, please," she pleaded as she sought her mother's approval.

A tear welled up in her mother's eye as she contemplated the situation. Finally, she spoke. "Let her be happy, Giuseppe."

Jean's father was silent. From the corner of his eye, he thought he saw Joe smirking.

"All right, but you must wait until the next time Joe is on leave. Do not rob your mother of a wedding. These things take time to plan."

"Thank you, thank you, Papa," she kissed him, and then turned to hug her mother. A tear rolled down her mother's cheek. Tears of happiness, Jean thought.

Joe shook Giuseppe's hand, but he was seething beneath his cool exterior. He saw it as defeat. "That old bastard," he thought. "If it wasn't for him, I'd be going on my honeymoon."

Joe would not wait past six months. "Let's get married on my birthday," he pleaded. "That is the best present you could ever give to me."

The wedding was simple and elegant with a lavish church ceremony and a family dinner. Jean's mother cried throughout the service, not because she was happy but because Joe was taking her youngest daughter back to Michigan to live "off base" so he would have her close by.

"Why can't you stay with us until Joe returns from the service?" Jean's mother cried.

Jean saw it as an adventure. "I'll be fine," she assured her mother.

The train ride was exciting, and Jean forgot the sadness of leaving her family as she watched the towns go past the window, putting more and more distance between her and New York. Joe told her about the apartment waiting for her to make their home. Jean felt so grown up and couldn't wait to be a housewife. When she arrived in Michigan, Joe carried their suitcases up to the third floor of the Army assigned apartment. He carried Jean across the threshold and they spent their first night laughing and whispering until they fell asleep in each other's arms. But when she woke up, Jean found that Joe had already gone. She had forgotten that he had to report for duty first thing in the morning, and she felt very alone. She shook off the feeling and dressed to go shopping. Her list was long with food items. She looked around the kitchen and scribbled curtains onto her list. Stocking and decorating the small apartment kept her busy, and every night she cooked a full course meal for Joe, who came home exhausted. The first thing he wanted was a drink. Jean was so happy in her starched white apron that she did not notice the change in Joe. His drinking made him moody and argumentative.

Jean's happiness was short-lived. She found herself alone most of the time. When Joe was home, he drank and complained about how he was treated on the base until she dreaded his return at the end of the day.

"I miss my sisters," she sighed one night. She was startled by the crashing glass that hit the wall and just missed her.

"I don't want to hear about your family," he screamed, getting up to fix himself another drink.

"I want to go home," she cried.

"You are home!" Joe yelled then walked out the door, leaving Jean to cry herself to sleep.

Joe stayed at the base for two days. He returned with flowers and an apology. He expected a night of reconciliation, but Jean was cool to his touch.

"I've decided to go back to New York. I want to see my mother. I'm leaving this week, but I won't be gone long," she promised. But Jean had no intention of going back. After a month, Joe began to get angry. He called her everyday and begged her to come back, but she refused. Joe began to drink a lot. The alcohol brought out his bad side—the side that was like his father, the side he swore he would never submit to. Overcome with anger, he started getting into trouble on the base, drinking and fighting with anyone who rubbed him the wrong way. He called and screamed at her to come back. "You're my wife," he reminded her. "Why did you marry me if you don't want to be with me? If you don't come back on your own, I'm coming to get you," he warned.

Jean feared what would happen if she didn't. His daily threats became desperate.

"I don't want to be alone for the holidays. Come back, now," he demanded. "Please come back. I miss my mother and I'm so lonely."

Jean began to soften.

"Don't leave," her mother begged. "I may not be here when you come back."

"What are you saying? I will only be gone a few weeks," Jean promised.

Jean's mother sadly waved goodbye to her youngest daughter from the front porch as she left for the train station. Looking into the side mirror as the car pulled away from the curb, Jean watched her mother disappear. The vision of her mother's face that morning haunted Jean for the rest of her life.

* * * * * *

Joe did not know Jean had no intention of staying in Michigan until they drove home from the station. He thought that he had won, and his wife was back for good.

They argued all night and by morning, Jean was exhausted. Startled by the phone, a shiver ran down her spine before she picked up the receiver. It was her uncle. "Your mother is sick. You need to come home."

Jean wanted to take a plane, but Joe insisted they didn't have enough money. "The train will take you just as fast," he assured her.

Jean found herself back on the train. When she arrived at the station, she knew something was wrong.

"I want to see my mother," she told her uncle. "Take me to the hospital now."

His silence caused her to feel sick to her stomach and she knew she was too late. As they pulled up in front of the funeral home, she realized what was happening.

"No, no, no! I want my mother!" she screamed.

"I'm sorry, Jean," her uncle consoled. "Your mom died on Thanksgiving Day. We didn't want to tell you on the phone. She is being buried tomorrow."

The world turned black for Jean. She could not speak. Her uncle held her up as she walked into the funeral home to view her mother for the last time. Her legs stopped working and her brain shut down. Her mother was gone and nothing else mattered. Blaming herself, she was convinced that her mother died of a stroke due to the news of a train crash she heard about on the radio Thanksgiving morning, thinking her daughter was on the train. After the funeral, she shut herself in the small room that used to be her bedroom.

Jean's family tried to protect her, but they could not help her through the grief. Jean refused to go back to Michigan after the funeral. She clung to her sisters, especially Lucia, who was now also married.

Jealousy consumed Joe when he realized that he could not convince Jean to come back to Michigan. He had no choice but to wait until he was discharged from the Army. He reluctantly agreed that she could stay in New York until he came back home, but he could not let go of his anger as he packed his belongings and returned to the barracks on base.

Animosity was in the background of their correspondence, each with their own reasons for thinking their marriage was a mistake. Previous words of warning from her mother not to marry Joe became the cement that sealed Jean's emotions.

Jean blamed Joe for her loss and never forgave him. She remained in her father's house, confused about her life and her marriage. She wanted a divorce, but she was afraid of how Joe would react. She thought it best to wait until he was out of the Army.

"I'm here suffering while you live the good life," he accused. "You are at your sister's house every night. What are you doing all hours of the night with your sister and her husband?" Joe's imagination went wild when he could not reach Jean by phone. She didn't want to confront his anger, which grew with the infrequency of their long-distance conversations. It was easy to pretend that he didn't exist. She put up an emotional wall that inflamed Joe's jealous nature.

Jean began to hide her visits to Lucia and her frequent entries in local talent shows. She loved to sing and found that she was quite good. When she won first place at the talent show, a talent agent approached her. "I would like you to come down to my studio," he urged, handing her his business card. "I think you have something special." Jean was flattered. She hid the card in her wallet and dreamed of becoming famous. She promised to come by, but knew that it was impossible. Joe would never allow her to pursue such a career. She kept her activities to herself. It was easier than trying to explain to Joe.

Joe drank heavily and took out his aggression by fighting whoever was in his way. "I don't want you at the dances, and don't even think about singing in some club," Joe wrote from his barracks. He was still angry that she left him and moved back to her father's house. He had to give up their apartment and return to the base.

Jean took a job in the financial district of New York City as a secretary. She saved all her money, hoping that someday she could buy her own house. In her new skirt suit and hat, she walked up the avenue on Wall Street. Important people passed and greeted her with "Good morning!" as she hurried to her forty-seventh floor office. She loved the feeling of independence and purpose. Jean was so happy that she almost forgot she was married.

******

Joe stared out the window of the train as it traveled toward home. His wallet was fat with the money given to him by the Army. Visions of his mother flashed through his mind. If she were alive, he would have someone to show his award for honor and courage. He knew she would have been proud of her son. The train stopped with a jolt. The sudden stop shook him out of his trance and he exited onto the platform. As he passed, people nodded when they saw him in uniform. It felt good, but he had served his time and was now free. The first thing he did was to visit his old friends.

Jimmy, known as Prunes to Joe, was already married with two young girls and another baby on the way. Joe didn't care for Prunes' wife, Beth. She purposely tried to keep them apart, thinking that Joe was a bad influence.

"Joe! When did you get back?" Prunes hugged his friend then punched his arm playfully. "Come on in!"

"I just got in today and I needed to see my drinking buddy. What do you say we go down to McAllister's bar and catch up on old times?"

Beth held her swollen belly and silently stood in the doorway, waiting for her husband to look her way.

"No, Joe. I can't leave Beth in her condition," Prunes apologized.

One of the babies began to cry and Beth went to check on her. "She's a little colicky," he told Joe. "She keeps us up all night, right, Beth?" He took the baby out of Beth's arms and tried to soothe her.

"Jimmy isn't going out drinking with you tonight, Joe," Beth said.

"Yeah, it's not a good time. Maybe next week," Prunes promised.

"Okay, Prunes. Give me a call and we'll get together," Joe said as he left the apartment, but he knew that it would not happen.

Joe drove over to Tony's house. His father answered the door and stared at Joe in his uniform.

"Tony doesn't live here anymore," he said, slamming the door in Joe's face. Disappointed, Joe realized that things changed since he left.

Finally, Joe appeared at Jean's father's front door. Phyllis let him in, but she wasn't happy. Joe's return meant that Jean would have to leave soon, but she was just starting to deal with their mother's death.

"Jean, come out here," Phyllis called to the bedroom. "There's someone here to see you."

Jean could not believe her eyes. Dressed in a very expensive cashmere coat, Joe reached out to hug her. He excitedly showed off the new car he bought with the money Uncle Sam gave him upon his discharge.

"How long have you been home? Why didn't you call me?"

"Aren't you happy to see me?" Joe accused.

Jean's family was furious. They did not like Joe and thought it was selfish of him to spend all his Army earnings on himself, but they kept their mouths firmly shut. Jean reluctantly gave him her money so they could rent a small apartment in Flatbush. It was only three miles away from Bensonhurst, but Jean was sad to leave her family again. Joe and Jean fought every night and every day about her spending too much time with her sisters.

"I don't want their help," Joe yelled, when Jean told him they gave her money. Joe was not having luck finding a job. He applied for a position as a mechanic whenever he saw a gas station, but usually ended up at the bar before the end of the day. He was reluctant to leave the apartment for fear his wife would run off to her family. At night, he drank at dinner and didn't stop until they were screaming at each other.

"I can't have you disturbing my other tenants," the landlord complained after a turbulent night of fury. "I'll give you one last chance."

Jean tried to defuse her husband's anger, but after a few drinks, nothing could hold back the dike. When the landlord threw them out, they were forced to find another apartment. Joe found a job in Rockaway as a grease monkey in a gas station.

"I know of a woman two blocks away who is looking for a tenant," Joe said. It was only sixteen miles away from Flatbush, but it felt like another state to Jean. She could not refuse because Joe secured the place for a reduced rent. But there was a catch. Jean was expected to help with the housekeeping and maintenance of the main house while Jean and Joe lived in the basement. Jean sank into a depression. Her exhaustion from working all day and fighting all night made her careless. She turned on the burner beneath a frying pan filled with olive oil. At the same time, Joe came in from work.

"Did you get paid?" Jean asked.

Joe handed her some bills he dug out of his pocket.

"Is this it? Where is the check?"

"I cashed it," Joe replied, walking into the bedroom.

Jean followed. "What did you do with the money?"

"You have it!"

Jean knew that he only gave her a small portion of his earnings, but had no way to prove it. As they argued, she froze. "What is that smell?"

They both ran into the kitchen, now blazing with fire. Jean panicked and threw a pot of water on the flames. The flames jumped out in anger and devoured the curtains above the stove. She left Joe with the fire and ran upstairs to get help. By the time the fire department came, there was not much left of the kitchen.

Jean's sister called and told her about an empty apartment in Brooklyn. Joe went to sign the lease. Jean was pleased with herself as they packed their belongings to move, but her joy did not last long.

She went upstairs and sat at the landlord's kitchen table, waiting for her husband to come back from Brooklyn. Joe was gone a long time. The look on his face when he came through the door alerted Jean that there was a problem.

"I have bad news," Joe told her. "We did not get the apartment because someone else put money down on it first."

"What are we going to do?" Jean worried.

"I spoke with my father and he said we could move into my old room at the house."

"Oh, god! No! I don't feel good. I need to sit down." Jean sat on the chair holding her stomach. "I feel nauseous," she said, then ran into the bathroom. After vomiting, she washed her face and went back into the kitchen.

"I thought you didn't want to be around your family!" she said.

"I don't, but we have no choice. It will only be for a little while until we find a place."

Jean did not want to go and made every excuse to prevent it.

"We could borrow money from my father," she begged him.

Joe refused, leaving Jean heartbroken and defeated as he

carried the suitcases to the car. She jumped from the kitchen fire to the frying pan. They moved in to Joseph's house and Jean tried to make the best of it.

Their room was small and the walls were thin. She was used to her husband's jealous rages and the fights that occurred without warning, but now the fighting happened all around her. The walls shook as Dom beat his wife in the next room. Tori's cries sent shivers down Jean's spine. Forced to sit and listen, she was powerless to help her new sister-in-law.

"We need to stay out of it," Joe warned.

Thunder in the halls erupted when the twins beat each other after a night of drinking.

"You son-of-a-bitch," Dom snarled, and Jean heard the sound of fists on flesh.

Jean tried to remain as quiet as possible. "Maybe they'll think no one is home," she thought as she waited for Joe to get home from the pool hall.

When Joe finally came home, Jean ran to him. "I don't want to live here," she cried. "I'm packing my stuff and leaving, with or without you."

Joe knew she meant it and didn't know what to say. He didn't want to lose his wife.

"Give me one week to find us another place," he promised. She reluctantly agreed.

One week turned to two, then three. Jean was sick every day. She thought it was stress and tried to ignore it, but her sister insisted that she see a doctor. Lucia sat in the waiting room reading a magazine. After a long time, she walked over to the receptionist window and peeked through. A nurse was helping her shaky sister out of the exam room.

"What's wrong?" she cried as soon as Jean joined her.

"I'm in trouble."

"Are you sick?"

"No, no. Nothing like that."

"What is it?" Lucia became frantic.

"I'm pregnant!"

Lucia put her arms around Jean and they both began to cry.

"I can't bring a baby into that house. What am I going to do?"

Joe did not take the news well either.

"How did this happen," he asked, as if he had nothing to do with it. They argued, giving Joe an excuse to walk out the door and spend his evening at the bar.

Jean realized that she could never be happy with Joe. She wanted a divorce! When Joe returned, he found a note from Jean.

"Our marriage was a mistake. I am going home to my father!"

Joe ripped up her note and passed out on the bed. "Good riddance!" he thought. After a few days, he had a change of heart, but every time he called Jean on the phone, she hung up.

Crying outside her father's house, he begged her to come out and talk to him. When he started getting agitated, her aunt begged Jean to go out to him before he came in.

Giuseppe took pity on him. "It's hard to bring up a baby on your own," he told his daughter. "You should go back to your husband."

Jean slipped out the front door and confronted Joe.

"I'm sorry," he cried. "I love you. Please give me another chance!"

"I'm not going back into that house," she swore.

"I'll get an apartment."

"You get a place for us to live and I'll consider it," she reluctantly agreed.

Joe promised to be the best husband and father in the world. He wanted to make sure that his child did not grow up the way he did. "We'll call him Joseph if he is a boy or Florence if she is a girl," he insisted.

"Oh, no," Jean cried. "If the baby is a girl, I am naming her after my mother. There are enough Florences in the family from your brothers and sister."

"It can be her middle name: Anna Florence Fuccino."

"No," Jean insisted. "I don't want my first daughter to have that name."

Joe could not change her mind. He accepted the name and tried to smooth things out with his family.

When Jean went into labor, Joe did not know what to do. He called his sister who told him to relax. "The first baby takes time," Dolly said. "It is going to take hours for her to give birth. I'll come and sit with her if you like."

After twelve hours, Dolly was frantic. "The baby is not dropping," she announced.

Dolly pressed on her sister-in-law's belly, thinking she could move the baby downward. Nothing! She tried to sit on her stomach, but Jean's screams caused her to back off. Hours went by, and Joe held his head to muffle out his wife's cries.

"Please call my sisters," Jean begged.

Joe did not want to call and waited until panic set in. By the time Lucia and her husband arrived at the house, Jean was silent.

"Are you trying to kill my sister?" Lucia cried.

"What are you doing here?" Joe asked.

"I'm here for my sister. Help me carry her to my car."

Joe hesitated for a moment before helping his brother-in-law carry Jean to his car. He hated Jean's family, but this was no time to argue. At the hospital, Joe waited outside the delivery room, cursing his in-laws for making him look bad. But his anger melted away when the nurse told him he had a little girl.

Jean spent seven days in the hospital. She was happy to be a new mom and quickly forgot the pain of childbirth. Her family came everyday to visit and bring gifts for the baby and Jean. Joe thought they were intruding on his happiness. He said little, but the look on his face told Jean that he was only tolerating her sisters for her.

The joy of fatherhood softened the pain buried deep inside of Joe. He insisted that the crib be near the window of the small apartment where he and Jean lived. He wanted his child to look out on the garden. She was only a baby, but he wanted to surround her with beauty. His landlady came to visit everyday to hold his daughter, Anna. Josephine, the landlady, had been very close to Joe's mother.

"I wish your mom was here to see her grandchild," the old Sicilian lady said, looking up to the sky. "I am kissing your granddaughter for you, Florence." Joe felt his throat tighten as he held back the tears. Italian people are often very emotional, and it didn't take much to make him cry.

Joe hated to leave his baby when he left for work everyday, but Jean was happy! She spent her days dressing her new baby in the finest clothes. She tucked Anna into the carriage and walked down to Eighteenth Avenue, where she met her sisters for lunch. Lucia pushed her baby carriage to face Jean's, so their daughters could look at each other. Mary's two girls sat politely at the table while Phyllis's two boys ran wild, causing their mother to yell constantly.

"These boys are driving me crazy! I wish I would've had girls," she cooed to Lucia's daughter. After lunch, they strolled together along the busy avenue, window shopping and losing time, then dashing back home to cook dinner for their husbands. Sometimes they packed their children up and took the train to Coney Island to spend the summer days near the boardwalk. The four sisters enjoyed their time together, but it was different when their husbands were around. The men tolerated each other, but tempers ran high and they looked for excuses to avoid getting together.

"I didn't like what your sister's husband said to me last night," Joe complained.

"Oh, he didn't mean anything."

"I don't care. I don't want him in my house anymore."

The sisters constantly tamed their husband's aggressions so they would not be separated, but it wasn't easy.

A Gift

Love can be pleasure, love can be pain,
And yet we do it again and again.
Mother Nature created this feeling,
It's giving a gift and the taker is stealing.

Hours are spent on sorrow alone,
This you will find where ever your roam.
Those who suffer are called a fool
Yet welcome it no matter how cruel.

Is it so foolish to feel great love?
Wasn't it created by the heavens up above.

— Gemini Joe

Chapter Eleven

Joseph kept a key in his stained shirt pocket at all times. Due to mistrust for the banking system and the fact that most of his money was illegal, he deposited his money in a green metal box under the stairs. He doled out the cash only when coerced. Between gambling proceeds and the high interest he collected on loans, he managed to accumulate some wealth. His children knew that he had money, but they could never figure out where he hid it. Each felt entitled to his or her fair share, but no one wanted to leave their separate apartments in the house. They stayed with their feet firmly planted in their places, screaming and cursing each other as fights spilled out into the hall. Joseph fought with them to pay their share of the living expenses through bitter words and threats.

"Get out of my house, you son of a bitch," Joseph yelled at Dom.

"Pack your bags and your wife, and get the hell out if you're not going to pay rent," he yelled at Franc.

Joe was glad that he didn't live in the house. It was bad enough that he lived on the same block. He never liked the fighting and didn't want to be dragged into his siblings' daily brawls. Even when the rent was paid, it wouldn't be long until Joseph's twin sons borrowed money, swearing they would pay it back, and laying the groundwork for another fight.

Dom and Franc frequently came up with business ideas for their father to fund, trying to emulate their father's business ingenuity. They convinced him to front the money for a mobile vegetable stand, promising to pay him back. But the fruits and vegetables they sold were hard to keep fresh, and soon the business folded.

They turned to door-to-door soliciting to sell ice cream they bought from the factory down the street.

"Pop, we need money to buy an ice-cream cart," Dom pleaded.

"What happened to the vegetable stand?" his father asked.

"You're not getting another dime out of me, you bastard."

Joseph's words fell on deaf ears because they didn't hold the weight of conviction. Arguments heated in the twilight of the day, but by morning Joseph backed down.

"Take the money and get out," he yelled.

Franc's smiling face emerged as he counted the money his father threw at him.

* * * * * *

Teresa appeared one day as if she had always been part of the family. She was a small Italian woman, physically frail, but strong minded. Her thinning, brown hair swirled into a bun at the top of her head in an attempt to hide her scalp. Teresa cooked Joseph his meals, regulated his medicines, and provided basic hygiene. No one questioned her relationship with Joseph out of respect for their dead mother. She was the only one he trusted with his finances. Teresa would leave the room whenever one of Joseph's offspring came to visit. The mysterious woman became invisible as she blended into the household, unheard and unseen.

As emphysema invaded Joseph's lungs, he found it hard to catch his breath and spent most of his time in his armchair. Dolly came to eat lunch with him everyday and kept him informed of the misdeeds of his sons, breeding resentment with her brothers. She sought protection from her brother's cruelty, fearing what would happen when her father died. Dolly voiced her concerns to her father, who sat and listened without response, his mind poisoned against his sons.

He rewarded her with cash for informing him about his sons. When he left the room to get his wallet, Dolly rose to her feet, careful to keep the floor from creaking, and tiptoed to the doorway, straining for a clue to her father's hiding spot and listening for his returning footsteps. Before she could discover her father's secret place, he lumbered back down the hall. She scurried back to her chair, looking innocent and bored.

* * * * * *

Joseph was disappointed with his sons, especially his youngest son and namesake. He expected the twins to be selfish and greedy, but not Joe, who visited only on special occasions and stayed only as long as their conversations were pleasant. As soon as he saw a fight coming on, he said his goodbyes. Sometimes Joe found himself in discussions that made him uncomfortable and he felt caught in his father's web.

"I'll show your brothers," Joseph growled. "They're not getting anything from me when I die."

"Please, Pop, make everything equal," Joe pleaded with his father.

"Why should I?" his father barked. "Do I look like I give a shit? My children don't respect me, and I'll do as I please."

"Don't you care about the family?" Joe asked.

"Enough! If it will get you off my back, I will draw up a will."

The next time Joe came to visit, he was surprised to see his father in a good mood.

"Joe," his father smiled. "Come and sit with me while I have my dinner."

Joe helped his father move his oxygen stand to the dining room table and handed him the hose in case he lost his breath. Joseph nodded to Teresa, who walked out into the hall. When she returned, she was carrying the green metal box. She laid it on the table and retreated to her room, leaving Joe alone with his father. Joseph opened the box and pulled out some legal papers, handing them to his son.

"Here, read this. I am naming you executor," his father said, reaching for his oxygen hose. "Now leave me alone!"

He stuffed the documents back into the box, but before it closed, Joe caught sight of the money. Stacks of thousand dollar bills lined the bottom of the box. He wondered just how much was in there and if anyone else knew about it. Joseph called for Teresa to carry the box back to its place. Joe left his father's house feeling more confident. "Maybe there is hope for my family," he smiled.

* * * * * *

Joseph spent the last month of his life sitting in a chair, stubbornly absorbing oxygen to keep his body from turning cold, but his heart was already frozen. Stone cold eyes peered out with contempt at those around him. The sins of his life lined his sallow face and the barbed wire stubble on his chin kept his grandchildren at a distance. He refused to let Teresa lather him up for his daily shave as he slipped beyond the land of the living. He preferred to focus his effort on breathing and saving his strength to combat his sons.

"You bastards," he mumbled. "I know you're all waiting for me to die, but I'm not going anywhere. You're all in for a surprise." Days turned into weeks, and Joseph's family started to believe that maybe their father could beat death, just by his sheer determination. Nevertheless, the devil finally got impatient and came to collect him one winter morning. The man that committed crimes against society and had little compassion for his family was dead.

News of Joseph's death spread, and his friends came to the funeral home to pay their respects. Dolly greeted the mobsters and thugs, who refused to sign the guest log. They slipped envelopes of condolences into her pocket book, and she looked around to make sure her brothers weren't watching.

The family followed his hearse, along with nine black limousines carrying his friends. The progression made its way to the cemetery, where Joseph's wife waited in the adjoining burial plot. After lowering Joseph's cold body into the ground and laying the final rose on his coffin, the family met back at the house for the reading of their father's will. They sat around the large dining room table in their father's apartment and waited for the lawyer to arrive. Teresa brought the metal box, which contained a copy of Joseph's will. Joe stared at the box on the table. It was grey!

I could have sworn it was green, he thought. Maybe the light had made him only think it was green. He couldn't be sure, so he said nothing. His father had promised to divide everything equally. But something inside Joe knew there was going to be a problem. As the lawyer entered the room to read their father's decree, Joe warned his siblings, "No matter what Pop put in the will, we are equal."

Dolly turned her eyes away from her youngest brother and remained unusually quiet.

Silence was rare among the family, but as the lawyer read the will, no one made a sound. He began by declaring the executor. Joe looked down, fearing how his brother's would react when he was named. Joe was shocked along with his brothers when the lawyer named Dolly.

"I was supposed to be the executor," Joe said in a low whisper. Joseph did not honor his promise. Instead, he made good on his threat to make them fight over his money. He bequeathed half of the estate to his daughter. The other half was to be divided among his three sons and companion, Teresa, after the lawyer and funeral costs were paid.

The snake ripped himself from six feet under the ground to bite them with his last words. Joe always knew his father had a vindictive streak but he had hoped that in the end, affection for his family would prove to be greater. The fighting is about to begin, Joe thought as he looked into the faces of his twin brothers. If he had been executor of his father's will, he would have had the power to change it. Now it was up to his sister. Dolly, who sat quietly during the reading, disappeared without a word. She locked her door once she was safely inside her apartment.

At first, disbelief paralyzed them as they sat around the table. As the sting lessened, voices began to rise. A volcanic eruption followed as Joe's brothers began to yell.

"This is not his will!" Dom screamed.

"Where is his original will?" Franc set his eyes on the old lawyer.

Joseph's counselor looked down at his portfolio, trying his best to avoid eye contact.

"Your father made a change to his will last month," he replied, twitching in his chair.

The lawyer could sense their tempers heating up and felt like a target while they looked for someone to blame. As the brothers discussed how they could fight the will, the lawyer discreetly packed his case and took the nearest exit. In all the commotion, no one noticed him leave. Once outside, he wiped the sweat from his brow with the starched white hankie he kept in his lapel pocket. Willing his old legs to move, he jumped into his car and drove off, not looking back for fear of seeing Joseph's angry sons in his rearview mirror.

"That old bastard!" Dom said, shaking his fist at the ceiling. They felt his presence looming above them. "I think our sister had something to do with this," Franc yelled, looking at Joe.

Joe tried to calm his brothers down. "It's a mistake. We'll work it out. I'll talk to Dolly," he promised.

No one mentioned the box. They were too busy fighting

over the injustice dealt to them by their father. When he realized that Teresa was no longer in the house, Joe decided he had better not mention it. He didn't want to risk making things worse. All the wealth Joseph had accumulated through the years was gone, along with Teresa and the green metal box under the stairs.

Time

To have been a fool of your yesterdays
And just a dreamer of tomorrows
Hinders all of your today's
Only to make a fool with sorrows.

The unobtainable is always much desired
To accept the past for what it was.
Should be the thought of today
For it will make tomorrow acceptable come what may

— Gemini Joe

Chapter Twelve

Nervous but determined to make peace in the family, Joe knocked on his sister's door. His niece opened the door and led him to the living room where Dolly and Tony sat whispering on the couch.

"Joe," she said defensively, "I didn't know! I swear!"

"We have a big problem, Dolly. You know the twins are not going to let this go without a fight," he warned his sister.

"I don't know what to do." She began to cry.

"I suggest you overturn the will," Joe counseled.

"I can't do that," she said, wiping her tears.

"Why not?" Joe looked puzzled. She was executor. She had the power.

"It was Pop's last wish and I will not go against him in his death. Besides, I was the only one who took care of him. Franc and Dom fought with him and you were never around."

"Dolly, what are you saying? Don't you realize what this will do to our family?"

"I'm sorry—I can't!" She turned and walked out of the room, leaving her brother stunned.

It only took a second for him to come to, and he jumped up and went after her. "Please, we need to make peace in our family. There's been too much fighting since mom died."

"You need to leave now, Joe," Tony said as he used his cane to lift himself from the couch. Joe always liked Tony and felt bad that he lost his leg in World War II. Tony never complained. He had been Joseph's right hand man, collecting debts and running errands. In return, Joseph reduced his rent.

"Give her some time to think about it," Tony insisted as he pushed his brother-in-law toward the door.

Joe left but he felt the rumblings of war deep below the

streets of Brooklyn. Sides were drawn. Caught in the middle, Joe did not know what to do. He considered himself a wimp when it came to family brawls. Just like when he was a child, he preferred to hide in a quiet place away from the yelling and screaming until the storm blew over. But this storm was going to do damage.

As the adults fought, their children fought too. Cousins passed each other on the street without acknowledging one another. Like strangers, they exchanged no words, refusing to go against their parents. Dolly remained hidden in her apartment while her angry brothers beat on the door day and night.

"Dolly, get out here. We want to talk to you."

She waited until they tired, staying quiet behind the door until they went away.

"I thought you were going to fix this!" Franc jeered at his youngest brother.

"Give her some time," Joe assured his brothers. "She'll do the right thing."

Joe almost believed it himself, but deep inside, he knew that he would have to persuade her. He waited a week then went back to his sister's apartment.

"Please, Dolly, let me in. I need to talk to you," he pleaded. "Franc and Dom hired a lawyer. They want me to sign on with them. I don't want to hurt you."

Through the silence on the other side of the door, he heard her body's weight on the creaking floor as she moved. He knew she heard him.

"Dolly, please," he begged.

As Joe turned to walk away, the door suddenly opened. He spun around and pushed through the doorway before his sister could change her mind.

"You need to share the house equally between us," Joe pleaded.

"You don't understand. I can't do that. Once I divide the house, our brothers will band together and demand we sell the house. My family will have no home. I can't let that happen. Dad knew! That's why he took care of it. Please don't side with Franc and Dom. I promise to take care of you if you support me."

"Dolly, you put me in a bad position. I don't want to fight and I can't stop the rest of you. I won't take sides, but I won't fight the will either. I suggest you sell this house and give them their shares. You can buy another house."

Dolly agreed that it would be best, but weeks turned into months. Dom lived in the apartment below, and Franc in the apartment above. They made life hell on earth for Dolly, but she wouldn't give in. Back and forth to court they went, with no resolution. Her brothers tried to have their father declared incompetent at the time he changed the will. But without proof that there was a previous will, the judge threw out the case.

"It was in that green metal box," Franc told Dom. "What ever happened to that?"

Joe refused to fight, and his brothers' wrath fell on him for not supporting them. Dolly kept her distance, knowing he would try to pressure her to share the house. Silence replaced the banging and threats, and her brothers made themselves scarce.

The children became silent as they passed each other in the halls and at school. Strangers living in the same house became a normal state of existence. Her nieces no longer shook the pictures on the living room wall with their bouncing balls. Dolly knew Franc and Dom were up to something and anticipated a storm, but she was unprepared for their next move.

"Dolly," her neighbor shouted as he knocked on her door, holding the local newspaper. "Are you selling your house?"

"No, of course not. What makes you ask such a thing?" she replied.

"Here," he said, pointing to legal announcement section in The New York Times. There it was, in the blackest of ink. An auction scheduled for that morning listed her house on the block. Dolly grabbed her coat and nearly knocked down her neighbor as she ran out. When she arrived at the courthouse, it was too late.

"Who?" she cried. "Who bought my house?"

She ran to each window begging the clerks for information. Her feet froze to the floor and she was unable to move when she saw her twin brothers laughing and slapping their lawyer on the back. After years of fighting, they found a loophole and went for the jugular. Dolly had not paid her taxes, and it didn't take long for a savvy lawyer to set things in motion for the government to take action.

She had thirty days to move her family and her belongings out of the house. She lost everything. Jean cried for her sister-in-law, but she did not want to get in the middle of the family's feud. She was glad that Joseph was dead, but she knew that Dolly was no match for her brothers. When the last stick of furniture was loaded on the moving van, Dolly entered the house one last time. The sounds of laughter came rushing back to memory as she recalled her youth. She could hear the music as they sat in the courtyard during the summer evenings when the family was young, when her brothers thought she was the most beautiful girl in the world. Quick to protect her honor back then, they would have killed anyone who caused her harm. She was the princess and her mother was the queen. The walls gave off the scent of her mother's perfume and Dolly breathed in deeply. "Mama," she cried. "I need you."

She could feel her mother's presence in every room. Florence was the only one who ever could control her father and brothers. She kept the peace through gentle guilt.

Tears streamed down her face as she passed one of her brothers in the hall. Silently, he walked without looking at his sister as if she were invisible, his noisy family following behind. Satisfied with their gains, they had no empathy for Dolly and her family. The family who had stuck together through so many bad times had splintered beyond repair.

* * * * * *

Franc and Dom felt that Joe betrayed them by not fighting alongside them.

"You should have been with us Joe," they said, when it was all over. "You don't deserve it, but here's your share of the inheritance, according to Pop's will."

"I don't want it," Joe bitterly told them, but took it anyway. God knows he needed it. He drove home in a daze. When he stopped the car, he found himself looking at his sister's apartment on the fifth floor of an old tenement building. The lights were on and he could see Tony limp past the window with his one good leg. He doesn't deserve this after serving our country, Joe thought. Slowly he exited the car and walked up the front steps into their hall. It was a long climb to their fifth floor apartment. Joe's feet seemed heavy as he put one foot in front of the other up the stairs. He stood in front of his sister's door, listening to the noisy family on the other side. Finally, he raised his hand and knocked. Silence! He knocked again.

He heard the thump, thump of Tony's cane as he came to open the door. "Hey, Joe," he smiled. "Look who's here," he shouted over his shoulder.

The family came rushing into the living room. "Uncle Joe!" his nieces greeted him.

"Come on in and have something to eat," Tony instructed him. "Come sit down and join us."

Dolly was quiet as her eyes met his. He did not speak but moved toward her as she remained in her chair.

"Here, Dolly, I want you to have my share," he said, placing the envelope in her hand.

"Joe," she said staring at the money inside. "I don't know what to say."

"I want you to have it, Dolly. I know Pop would have wanted it this way."

The mood around the table lightened and they shared a glass of wine. His sister insisted that he stay and eat, but Jean was waiting for him at home. Joe did not want to leave her too long, but neither did he want to seem rude. He picked at the plate of food they set in front of him and waited for his chance to leave. Finally, he rose from the chair. "I have to leave. Jean is waiting."

Dolly hugged her brother as he left. "Don't be a stranger. Come back next time with Jean."

Joe took one last look up at the apartment before he drove off. He knew he would not be back. He smiled as he started out on his way home. His sister's gratitude gave him a good feeling but it did not last. Somehow his brothers heard the news of his generosity and their anger was fierce. No longer would they acknowledge their baby brother. To them, he was dead. The words of their father rang in his ears as they went their separate ways. "I'll see you all fighting in the streets for my money." Joseph fulfilled his promise and destroyed the family.

Gemini Joe

The Sounds of a Waterfall

Man suffers pain of the body and dies…
but man can also die in a living body
He can die of a broken heart and many broken dreams

When you look upon a person and judge him and mark him,
Think also that deep in his heart he may be carrying many hurts
And disappointments

The silence that one may express from outside of himself
May be hiding the days inner roaring for the want of happiness

Like the sound of a great river that comes to a waterfall
As the winter descends silently man must worship God no matter
What may befall upon him

The way to mercy and goodness is not an easy road
There will be many temptations and traps and many days of fear
and want and anxious moments and anger

Many times a man will fall victim to evil
God knows man will fail many times
Whatever the outcome of man depends on man's believing
In a supreme being

Love of man to his fellow man is the road to the kingdom of God
If it is godly then men should overcome
It fully, but most pain is not from the hand of god but rather from himself

— Gemini Joe

Chapter Thirteen

The roots of Joe's character were tainted by his family's cruelty and callousness. His experiences left scars. It saddened him that his father fulfilled his threat to split up the family by causing them to fight over his illicitly achieved riches once he was gone. Joe could have used the money bequeathed to him, but he just didn't have the stomach to fight with his brothers. With a growing family of his own, Joe was determined to be a good provider, but one-eighth of the inheritance would have made a big difference.

Joe hated his job. At the end of the day, he was in a foul mood and accused Jean of wasting her day with her sisters. "I have to work everyday, while you are out there playing," he complained. Although he wanted a job as an auto mechanic, he worked at the Veteran's hospital. Times were tough and jobs were scarce, so he accepted the part-time position offered to veterans returning from the Korean War. Veterans agonized in rehabilitation, missing arms and legs in the amputee ward. Joe found it very depressing, but he used his creativity to fix their wheelchairs, adapting the vehicles to each soldier's personal mishap.

He used his misery as an excuse to have a drink or two. Jean nervously cleaned the dishes after dinner. She didn't like it when he drank. Joe seemed to change into a different person.

"I'm going to put the baby to bed," she said to remove her daughter from his path.

"Yeah," he grunted, "you do that."

The distance between Joe and Jean grew during that year. Sex was not enjoyable and unavoidable, especially when Joe came home drunk. But it was easier to give in rather than hear him complain all night. She loved it when he worked overtime, because he had no time to sit at the bar. He came home like a lamb and quietly crawled into bed.

Gemini Joe

One winter night, Joe took a cigarette break behind the Veteran's hospital. He heard the laughter of two boys sliding on the iced-over lake. Before he could give them a warning, one boy fell through. The other boy tried to help his friend but soon found himself in trouble, too. Joe didn't think about the danger. He ran to the lake and crawled onto the ice, pulling one boy at a time to safety. His bravery saved the boys from drowning but, after delivering them to the emergency entrance of the hospital, he never saw them again. When he returned home, his wife announced that they were expecting another baby.

Joe stood there with his mouth open, his mind spinning in all directions. Maybe it will be a boy, he thought. Wouldn't that burn my brothers who so far have only produced girls?

Jean was happy, but apprehensive. They were barely making ends meet with one child. Joe did side jobs repairing cars, but he drank most of his earnings. They moved to another apartment on 45th street. Jean had a very uneventful pregnancy, but one month before her baby was due, she decided to hang curtains. She wanted Joe to help, but he was not home much. Jean climbed onto a chair and stretched her arms to put up the rod. A shape pain ran through her body and she felt funny. The doctor told her to get off her feet until she delivered, so Jean retreated to her bed.

Jean's second baby entered the world breech first, and caused Jean so much pain that she thought she was going to die. Anna was only two when her new baby brother arrived. She loved him so much and treated him like a new doll, especially when Jean let her sit on the couch and hold him. The family celebrated, naming him Joseph, of course. Finally, there was someone to carry on the family name. Joe knew he had to find a bigger apartment and more money. Thirteen blocks away an apartment building needed a super. It didn't take much for Joe to convince his wife to move. After working all day, he took out the trash pails, mopped the marble floors, and did odd jobs for the tenants at night. In return, he received free rent and utilities. Everyone loved Joe as he went from apartment to apartment, fixing leaky pipes and unclogging toilets.

He remained at the Veteran's hospital at night, but fixed cars during the day. At first there wasn't much work, but after a few months, word of mouth brought him new clients. He was offered a job as an auto mechanic at a local gas station, and quit the Veteran's hospital job. Joe celebrated by bringing home a box of candy and flowers for Jean and a cherry lollipop for each of his children.

"Get a babysitter. We're going to the movies," he instructed his wife. Jean jumped at the chance to go out and called the teenager girl next door, who was happy to earn a few dollars. Joe and Jean laughed like newlyweds and Jean fed off her husband's happiness. She felt hopeful that her family was going to be all right. Joe's new job seemed to quell the unrest inside of his head and the fights seized for a while. He still cleaned the apartment building at night, but his flask was never far from his pocket. After a few drinks, his singing echoed through the halls. But the peace only lasted a couple of weeks.

After a night of heavy drinking, Joe jacked up a car to check an oil leak. He placed the device under the chasse and lifted it high enough to crawl under the car. The owner of the car stood over him, watching his every move and making Joe nervous. Joe did not realize that the device was improperly lined up and was stunned when he found himself pinned under the car. His legs were crushed, but no broken bones. Still, he was off his feet for a while and relied on Jean to wait on him hand and foot.

Two weeks later, Joe was back to his old self once more, mopping the hallway floors, drinking and fighting with his wife.

"Were you at your sister's house again today?"

"Yes. We took our father to the doctor then went back to Lucia's for lunch."

"You're spending too much time with your family," he yelled, slamming his fist down on the table. He resented the fact that she had a family and he didn't.

Joe's sister came to visit, but he missed his brothers. He heard that they were doing quite well and both bought houses, cars, and the finer things in life.

"I should have stuck with them," Joe thought to himself.

After scrubbing the halls and stairwells at night, Joe sat on the stoop in front of the apartment building, feeling sorry for himself. As he puffed on his cigarette, he heard a girl's voice call in distress from across the street.

"No!" she yelled. "Get off me."

Joe noticed a man struggling to get on top of the young girl.

He quickly ran across the street and jumped on the man, punching him in the head. The man ran down the block with Joe in hot pursuit. But Joe lost sight of him near a shopping area, and the man managed to get away. Joe ran back to make sure the girl was all right and found that someone had called the police.

"You could have been stabbed and you would have deserved it," the officer said to Joe. "Next time, mind your own business."

The girl Joe saved was the local rabbi's daughter who had left the synagogue late that night. The rabbi was very grateful and paid Joe a visit the next day. The rabbi blessed Joe for his kindness, and if babies were a blessing, it must have worked. Shortly after, Joe received the announcement that his third child was on the way. Joe smiled when his wife gave him the good news then went outside to cry. His son was only two months old. How did this happen? he asked himself. The pressure mounted as expectations rose, and Joe had to shoulder more and more responsibilities. He felt like he was suffocating and only one thing helped: a drink.

* * * * * *

Joe couldn't make money fast enough and took on more side jobs. Even though he had trouble breathing, he always ended up with jobs that required him to breathe the worst air in the world. Exhaust from mechanic shops filled his lungs with carbon dioxide, and the limited ventilation made him cough. Sulfuric acid, used in gold, copper and brass plating, emitted constant fumes at the plating company job he took. Joe couldn't breathe but he couldn't quit either job, so he toughed it out.

He watched as his brothers used their father's money to start their own businesses. Franc opened his own plumbing company and Dom bought a semi-truck to start a moving company. Neither Franc nor Dom would forgive Joe for not standing by them during the fight for their inheritance. He missed his brothers and watched them from afar. Joe buried his pain and used it as another excuse to drink. His brothers ignored his constant attempts to contact them, but he never gave up trying to keep in touch.

Joe's heart broke for Franc when he heard about the family tragedy that struck his brother to his knees. The short-lived happiness Franc felt when his oldest daughter gave him his first grandchild turned to despair. As was the custom during the 1960s, mothers often bundled up their babies and put them outside in carriages to get fresh air. It was his daughter's first baby, and she wasn't sure about putting the baby outside alone on that late November day.

"It's sunny," her mother said. "She'll be fine, and we can watch her from the window."

Franc's daughter wrapped a blanket in hospital fashion, and put another on top, tucking it into the sides. The baby was asleep so she went back upstairs, where she and her mother set the table for lunch. From time to time she peeked out the window to make sure the baby was all right, and each time, the baby had her eyes closed.

"Fast asleep," she said as she continued to visit with her mom.

They did not realize that a cold front was invading New York. Losing track of time, Franc's daughter suddenly jumped up and looked out the window. The baby was still asleep, but had a strange hue. She ran down the stairs, two at a time, and bolted to the courtyard in the back. Even before she picked up her baby, she knew something was wrong. The ambulance seemed to take forever as she rocked her baby back and forth waiting for the miracle workers to arrive. She sat, stone silent, with her mother in the hospital waiting room, her eyes firmly planted on the swinging door that lead to the emergency cubicle. Doctors rushed in and out of the room without making eye contact, and she knew in her heart that something was wrong.

The look on the doctor's face when he entered the waiting room was all it took for a slow, painful wailing to come from the depths of her soul. Her baby was not coming home with her, not now, not ever. The incident was ruled an accident, but the horror and loss was worse than any legal punishment a mother could endure. Franc's daughter was never the same after that, and blame rolled around the family like a medicine ball. Franc did not speak, he just cried. It was his first grandchild, and her death snuffed out his happiness like a black cloud covering the sun. He looked up to the sky and asked, "Why, Pop, why?" Convinced his father had a hand in it.

Joe realized having money didn't ensure an easy life so he continued working to support his growing family. Jean was eight and a half months pregnant and soon their third child would be born. Joe tried to keep his joy under control, not wanting his happiness to rub in the face of his brother's agony.

Dana was in a hurry to be delivered and popped out with minimal labor. Jean was overwhelmed, and Anna was left on her own, a cheerless, lonely child. She played in the halls that her father cleaned every night. She stared at her reflection in the mirrors that lined the walls, fascinated by the tunnel effect as she peered into her multiple images in the mirror. Anna played under the stairs where many of the residents, including her own mother, parked their baby carriages. Anna's mother was busy upstairs with her brother and new baby sister, Dana. Her father was never home, but it was a relief not to hear the fighting that woke her out of her dreams in the middle of the night. She had to leave the tunnels behind when her father took a job as a mechanic for Sears and Roebuck, replacing auto repairs for washing machines. It was a steady job with good benefits, but he still could not afford to buy his family a house of their own. He dragged his wife and children from one apartment after another, some with no heat or hot water.

In the middle of winter, Jean's children sat bundled with their coats and hats. The boiler was broken again and it seemed colder inside than out. "This is the third time this month," Jean complained to her sister. Tears flowed down her face as she watched her children huddle together in bed, trying to keep each other warm.

Jean's family saw her suffering, but could do little to help her, fearing her husband's wrath. One day, her sister Lucia called. "Jean, I found a brownstone for sale only ten blocks from you. It's a really good deal and maybe you could buy it."

Jean gathered her children and rushed to meet Lucia. Her children were already bundled up in their warm winter coats because the landlord shut off the heat again. It didn't take long to get to her father's house, where her sister still lived.

The three-bedroom brownstone was perfect. The front yard had a small court with a garden. There was a main entrance to the house and a private entrance to basement, with enough space to build an extra room. The entrance into the house had a stairway, leading up to an enclosed porch, and Jean imagined herself sitting on the stoop with her neighbors, talking and laughing. A big, shady pear tree sat in the middle of the fenced-in back yard, where Jean's children could play outside while she watched them from the kitchen window.

Jean's eyes darted from one corner of the house to the other with excitement as her children ran up and down the stairs, laughing and teasing each other. Then her face froze as tears welled up in her eyes.

"Why did you take me here?" she said to her sister. "You know I can't afford it on Joe's salary."

Lucia smiled. "You know I'm moving to Long Island soon. Dad can't stay by himself and he's refused to come with me. I can lend you the money for the deposit if you take Dad in to live with you. We can make him a room down in the basement and he could pay rent every month."

Jean couldn't believe her ears. She took one more look around before they left, and began planning how she was going to persuade her husband. She cleaned the apartment and fed the children before preparing Joe's favorite dinner. When she was finished, she sat by the window to wait for Joe to come up the walkway. Her heart pounded like a drum with the sound of every footstep as he lumbered up the stairway to their door. He was in a good mood and obviously sober, so she knew that she had a good chance.

"Joe, I found us a house today," Jean announced over dinner.

"That's great, but you know we don't have the money yet. I just started this job and it is going to take a year or two to get enough to put down."

"Please," his wife begged. "My family has offered to lend us money for the down payment." The words blurted out of her mouth before she could filter them. "My father wants to live with us, and I found a house with a room down in the basement. He will help with the mortgage payment."

Joe's pride began to bubble up to his lips as he prepared to argue, but a piece of steak in his mouth blocked the words. Jean knew what was coming. She took a deep breath and spoke faster to make her point before she was stifled.

"My babies are cold, and we can't stay here. This may be the only chance to own a house, and if we don't take it, our children will have nothing."

Joe stared at her from across the table, food still in his mouth. He could not swallow. As her last sentence rolled around in his brain, the scars left by his father were touched by her words. He wanted his children to have something in life, and he knew he couldn't do it alone. Without his own family to help, he would have to accept the help of her family.

"All right, I will think about it," Joe told his wife as they finished their dinner.

That night, he left his wife and kids to go down to the corner bar, but Jean didn't mind. She cuddled up to her three children, sleeping in one bed, and fell fast asleep with a smile.

One month later, they moved into the brownstone. Jean's heart was light. She couldn't stop smiling, and Joe drank a little less. His creative side kicked in and he started planning projects around the house. He loved the pear tree in the yard and decided to build a seat around the trunk so his family could sit under its branches in any direction. In early summer, the pears ripened and fell to the ground, covering the yard. The pears fell into the small pool Joe bought for his children, rotting and attracting flies and bees. He tried to fish them out everyday, but it was a mess.

"I'll give you a penny for each piece of fruit you pick up," Joe told his children.

All three children ran around the yard picking up the pears, and Joe thought himself clever. But soon the novelty wore off, and after getting stung by bees a few times, his children refused to pick up any more pears.

Joe also decided to build a porch in the back, right off of the kitchen, and wooden steps in front of his house. When Joe worked around the house, things got turbulent. His children's curiosity often put them in the position of abuse, since Joe exploded when things didn't go his way. It was always someone else's fault, and the nearest person usually got blamed. Everyone learned to disappear whenever they saw him pick up a hammer.

First, he tore up the stairs leading to the back yard to make room for the porch.

"How are the children going to get outside without stairs?" Jean cried.

"Shut up and leave me alone," Joe snapped. "I know what I'm doing."

Weeks went by, and still there was no way to get into the yard without jumping down onto a dirt mound. Joe could not get the dimensions right, so he put the project on hold and moved on to the front porch. He drew up the plan for a brick stairway, with sides wide enough to sit along. He brought home big bags of cement and collected bricks that he stole from construction sites around town. He piled them in the yard until he had enough to start the project. He tore down the stairs in the front of the house, leaving a large hole.

"Don't let the kids go near the front door," he instructed Jean.

The projects were not always as easy as they seemed, and the brick stairway was no exception. Joe quickly became frustrated as he worked, moving the materials from the back yard to the front. His three children were excited and ran from the back to the front, trying to get in on the action.

"Watch these goddamn kids," he yelled at his wife as he walked out the front door with a bag of cement on his shoulder. He fell six feet, right where the brick stairs should have been. Joe lay stunned, looking up at his wife in the doorway.

"It's your fault," he yelled. "If you were a good mother, I wouldn't have had to work and watch the kids at the same time."

He climbed out of the hole, showered, and took off for the bar, leaving the construction for another day—and the mess for his wife to clean up. He returned late that night, arguing and looking for a fight. His children hid at the top of the stairs, listening and praying that he would not harm their mother.

* * * * * *

Even though Joe always resented his father for drinking too much, he followed in his footsteps and dove right into a bottle. It was his solution to a life that he could not change. Joe felt safe as the alcohol numbed his pain and slowly eased his grip on reality. Some people get happy when they drink, some get silly, but some get angry, and Joe was one of those. Characteristics he inherited from his family fueled by a cynical outlook on life caused him to fight. He lost his mother, his father, his brothers, and sister. There was no one left to fight with except his wife.

Joe's jealous tirades became a daily occurrence, fueled by resentment for his wife's sisters, who were constantly at his home. He tried his best to make them feel uncomfortable. When that didn't work, he came home from the bar and fought with his wife long into the night. Everyone loved him at the bar, he was a funny guy. But he was a different person when he was home.

Joe was anything but funny to his daughter, Anna. He often used her to make other people laugh. On her confirmation day, she felt special in her beautiful, white dress. While preparing the celebration dinner, Jean told her husband to take Anna to the park for pictures.

"Smile," he instructed, but his daughter's mouth remained stiff. Joe was getting angry and Anna could see that things were not going to go well. She quickly thought up an excuse, telling him that she forgot to brush her teeth and could not smile.

"She wouldn't smile because her teeth were dirty!" he joked to the family relatives. "She probably wouldn't walk if her feet were dirty." Everyone laughed—everyone, except Anna. She sat horrified as he made fun of her.

* * * * * *

Joe was ecstatic when two of Jean's sisters moved to Long Island, and didn't even mind her going to visit on the weekends. Only one sister remained, but she was no problem because her husband kept her close to home. Jean missed her sisters, especially Lucia. They had met at each other's houses for lunch everyday while their husbands were at work, spending hours talking, laughing, and closing out the rest of the world. But now Lucia was too far away to visit often, and Jean only saw her sister a couple of times each month. Loneliness ate a hole in her heart, and her eyes began to focus their gaze to the East.

All Jean had left were a few friends who gathered together for a weekly card game. Every Friday night, they met at Eleanor's house to play Canasta. Joe did not approve, but they were childhood friends and it was hard to argue, since he spent most of his nights at the bar with his friends.

On Friday night, Jean's friend, Betty, mentioned that her sister was selling her house on Long Island. She knew that Jean missed her sister. "You should go check it out, Jean. I think you would like it."

Jean took the information and tucked it away in her purse. She had to think of a way to broach the subject to her husband, but she knew her time was limited.

She waited for the right moment to bring up the subject, but there never seemed to be a right time. Until a few days later, Joe heard a loud knock at the front door. He ran to open it.

"Joe, I need to talk to you about your son," his neighbor shouted. "He has been hitting my daughter and you better make it stop. If you don't, I will kick his ass!"

Joe's heart began to beat in double time. He never liked confrontation and did his best to avoid it, but now it was at his front door and there was nowhere to hide.

"What? He's only ten years old," Joe responded, shocked, trying to gather his wits. "You better not touch my son."

"What are you going to do, you son of a bitch!"

"I'll kick your ass!" Joe couldn't believe the words coming out of his mouth.

"Oh yeah, well why don't you come out here right now and we'll settle it," his inflamed neighbor yelled.

"I don't want any trouble with you," Joe said.

"I knew you didn't have it in you. Well, teach your kid that he shouldn't go around hitting girls," he yelled as he turned to leave. "Or I'll be back."

Jean stood in the hallway with her children, unsure if she should call the police. When the front door closed and the neighbor crossed the street, she herded the kids to the living room. Joe stood in the doorway, his eyes squinting with anger. "Why weren't you watching your son?" Joe yelled at Jean.

"Why don't you tell your son not to hit?" Jean yelled back.

Joe turned to his son. "Don't hit girls anymore." Then he walked out the door and drove off. Joe tried to avoid his neighbor by spending more time at the bar and less time at home. The back porch remained unfinished while Joe stood out in the yard for hours staring at the dirt hole. Jean noticed that he seemed stressed, but did not know if it was because of the drinking, the porch or the neighbor. When he seemed on the verge of a breakdown, she took the opportunity to mention the house on Long Island. To her surprise, he eagerly agreed that they should move. The house was perfect! They had to reduce the price of their house in Brooklyn because it had no back porch, but they had enough for a large deposit for the colonial house on Elm Street in Long Island.

From the moment the moving truck pulled up in front of the house, Jean knew that she was finally home. Joe was excited too, and for a moment, he began to show his joy. He immediately began making plans to renovate, which worried Jean because Joe had a habit of incompletion. Neighbors came by to welcome them and he didn't mind the intrusion of Jean's family.

"Joe, I hope that you are registered as a Republican," said Al, the neighbor across the street. "Long Island is not like the city. Everyone around here is Republican. When you are ready, I will take you along to one of our meetings."

Joe nodded, basking in the new feeling of belonging, and promised that he would come once he was settled in. The glow dimmed after a week and he slipped back into old habits. "I have to commute to the city everyday now. I hope you're happy!"

Jean ignored his complaints. She loved her new home and being close to her family once more. Joe's concerns did not matter to her. Jean accepted a job at the local bakery to pay for the furniture on lay-a-way. Piece by piece, she worked to furnish her new home.

Joe's father-in-law, Giuseppe, did not want to leave Brooklyn, but he had no choice; he was too old to live alone. He packed his bags for Long Island and took a small room on the first floor of his daughter's new house on Elm Street. He was not used to the country, but it didn't take long before he was glad to be there. He loved the yard and sat under the oak tree everyday listening to the birds. The country air was sweet and the sound of crickets in the night lulled him to sleep. Circling sea gulls were a reminder that the ocean was not far away.

Janet Sierzant

Thoughts of Peace

Whenever I am troubled
And lost in deep despair
I bundle up my troubles
And go to God in prayer

I tell him I am heartsick
And lost and lonely too
My mind is deeply burdened
I don't know what to do

I know he stilled the tempest
And calmed the angry sea
I humbly ask if in his love
He'll do the same for me

I close my eyes in silence
Think only thoughts of peace
And in the midst of stillness
My restless murmurings cease

— Gemini Joe

Chapter Fourteen

Shortly after they moved into the house, Joe began the construction of a room in the basement for his father-in-law. Giuseppe hoped he would take his time, but Joe had another idea. He wanted to get the old man into the basement as soon as possible, and worked every weekend on the renovation. In the middle of the dark gloomy underground, next to the furnace and across from the washer and dryer, he cleared just enough space to make it livable, promising to heat it before winter. He put a bed and a television set in one corner and a kitchen area in the other, with an oven, refrigerator, a table, and chairs. Joe made sure the kitchen was functional, so his father-in-law could cook for himself. Giuseppe was only welcome to have dinner upstairs with the family on Sundays and holidays. Giuseppe took most of his meals in his small kitchen in the basement, where he could hear his daughter fighting with her husband above him.

"Jean, it's all right," he told her. "I like to eat downstairs. Please don't fight with your husband over me."

Jean saw that her father was not happy. He lied to make her feel better. Her heart was breaking, but she promised not to push the issue. Joe had no empathy for the old man, and Jean knew that she couldn't change his mind.

The minute Joe left for work Jean called her father to come upstairs for coffee and to warm himself. The first winter was cold, and Joe did nothing to heat the chilly, damp basement. Jean lay in bed, worrying about her father downstairs.

"I want a divorce," Jean announced, one night after dinner. "I'm tired of the way you treat me and my family. I want you out!"

Joe was stunned. He wasn't sure if it was the liquor that was making him hear things.

"What did you say?" He asked her.

"You heard me. I'm going to see a lawyer this week."

Before Jean could get to a lawyer, Joe arranged for them to go to marriage counseling. He would not let her kick him out of his house. Joe promised to stop drinking and treat her better, if only she would give him another chance. She reluctantly agreed to try and work out their problems. After a few sessions, the marriage counselor suggested that they sign up for a marriage retreat. They packed up their children and sent them to different relatives while they were gone. During the retreat, they had group and individual counseling and they were required to write each other letters, which were discussed during therapy. For the first time, Jean and Joe connected on an emotional level. Joe was sensitive and sober. Jean was forgiving and loving. They returned home with a new outlook on their marriage and their family, determined to make things work.

Their second honeymoon lasted long enough for Jean to get pregnant. The news of his wife's pregnancy gave Joe reason to celebrate, but Jean was not as happy. It had been ten years since she last changed diapers, and her children were finally old enough to take care of themselves.

"How can I have another baby?" she cried to her sister. "I'm too old!"

* * * * * *

When the forth child was born, Joe was determined to be a better father. He was amazed when she was born with blue eyes and blonde hair. His suspicious mind began to churn as he joked, "Who is she, the ilkman's daughter?" The seed of doubt was sewn, and his eyes studied the baby girl when no one was around. Still, Linda was the love of his life. Joe doted on her, ignoring his older children and pinning all his hopes and dreams on her.

Gemini Joe

Peaches and Cream

Little girl of peaches and cream
That one could find easy to love
Little girl with such a dream
Beauty of a snow-white dove

How great it would be in this life of ours
A lesson of love complete
If we could share this special dream
Lessons from a little girl so sweet

Linger now for a little while
Thoughts of what one could dream
Change your ways or even your style
And share the joy of peaches and cream

— Gemini Joe

Giuseppe loved the baby, and Jean was happy to put some joy into her father's life. Every morning he came upstairs to play with his granddaughter while Jean did her chores. One morning when she called down to her father, he did not answer. Jean found him shivering in his bed, burning with fever.

After finding someone to watch the children, Jean and Lucia followed the ambulance to the hospital. Jean stayed by his side late into the night until the nurses persuaded her to go home and get some rest. Her husband wasn't home when she crawled into bed and fell fast asleep.

Joe was still at the bar when the phone woke her in the middle of the night. Her father took a turn for the worse, but she could not leave the children. She waited till morning, found a sitter then rushed to his hospital. But it was too late, he was already gone.

When Jean returned home, Joe was sitting at the table.
"I'm sorry," he said when he saw the agony on his wife's face.
Jean snapped.
"How dare you?" she yelled. "You never cared about my

father. You treated him like a dog, and I will never forgive you."

It did not take Joe long to go back to his old habits. He left the house after dinner each night and did not return until everyone was asleep. Jean cursed her husband for his cruelty and turned a cold shoulder to him in bed, which inflamed him, so he spent more and more time at the bar. Coming home in a drunken stupor, he expected her to give him love. But the smell of alcohol and cigarettes turned Jean off, and she pushed him away.

Joe's children learned to be very quiet when he was in the house. The slightest noise or commotion, even the sound of a closing cabinet or a spoon dropping to the floor, sent him into an uproar. "What's going on? Goddamn it! I can't think! Where's your damn mother? You kids are destroying the place. Do you want a hammer?" An expression he used frequently when he thought his children were wild. He could not handle chaos around him and had little patience. His children, although hurt by the insinuation that they destroy things, accepted the insult and his intolerance of them, but it was a black mark against him.

Holidays were the worst. Joe couldn't go to the bar because it was closed. He started the day with his burgundy wine but, by evening, the scotch came out and he drank one glass after another. His family always ended up barricaded in the bedroom while he banged and yelled outside the door.

* * * * * *

Joe woke up early to commute to the city for his job at Sears and Roebuck as a washing machine repairman. At the end of the day, he pulled his truck into the garage and unloaded an old washing machine that one of his customers discarded. It was against the rules of the company to take the old washers when they delivered the new, but Joe did not care. He saw it as a way to make extra money, fixing and selling them for quick cash, which he pocketed and kept away from his wife.

Joe stayed at home only long enough to eat dinner, and then he was gone. "I'm going to the store to buy a pack of cigarettes," he told his wife, but she knew he wouldn't be home until late, and he wouldn't be sober.

Jean was glad Joe didn't spend much time at home. He called her "pinhead" when he was nice and "cunt" when he was drunk. Although they didn't know what it meant until they were older, his children were hurt when they heard it because they knew it was a bad word. Jealousy crept into Joe's thoughts whenever Jean occupied herself with things that did not include him. He hated sharing her attention with her sisters, her friends, and even his children.

Jean decided to get a job, partly because they needed the extra money, but mostly to get out of the house. Jean's friend convinced her to apply for a waitress job at the restaurant where she worked. "I make a lot of money in tips," she told Jean. "Sometimes, I come home with fifty dollars in cash."

Joe did not like the idea and tried to discourage her, but the thought of making her own money appealed to Jean. He hoped that she would get tired of working and quit, but Jean seemed to be happier everyday she left for work. Joe began to get suspicious. He imagined that she was off with a lover or busy looking for one. He constantly drove past The Pancake Cottage to check on her, peeking through the window to see what she was doing and who she was talking with. His jealous rages were worse after a night of drinking.

After an evening of spying outside the restaurant, Joe saw her laughing and talking to a man sitting at the counter. He could feel his blood rush to his head as he watched the man smile at his wife. It was almost time for her to leave, so he returned home to wait. A gallon of burgundy wine sat on the kitchen table, and he drank one glass after another as he worked himself up for a fight.

Tired from working all evening, Jean slipped into the small colonial house they shared on Long Island. She tried to steady the creaking of the screen door as it opened, but Joe's voice met her in the hall before she could make it to their bedroom to change out of her uniform.

"I know you were flirting with all the men in that restaurant tonight," he slurred. "That's how you get extra money, isn't it? Well, you could just fork over some of that right now."

"No," Jean quietly replied. "I need this money to buy the children clothes for school. You're not getting it."

His icy stare alerted her to the danger ahead. He belted back his drink, slamming the empty glass on the table.

"No," she repeated louder. "This is my money! I worked for it!"

Joe knocked over the chair as he jumped up from the table. He lunged toward her, but she, sober and quicker, made it out the front door just ahead of Joe. Jean felt him close behind. She soon found herself facedown on the lawn as he tackled her to the ground. The weight of his body had her pinned. She struggled as he tried to take the money from her apron pocket. Keeping her hands under her body, she managed to retrieve the bills before he could, clawing at the earth to bury her earnings. He was furious at finding her hands empty, and too drunk to see what she did with the money. In Joe's confusion, Jean was able to crawl away.

His children sat at the top of the stairs, listening as their father shouted in a drunken rage. Foul language spilled out of his mouth. The anger behind his words terrified them. He was hurting their mother. Just when they thought they could not hate him anymore, he began to cry. He cried that he was sorry he cried that no one loved him, and he cried because he made things worse. His children were disgusted, but glad that he was no longer a threat to their mother. They felt no pity for their father, but they had to pretend.

"I know that you think I'm the bad guy. She has turned my own children against me."

"Daddy, it's okay. We love you."

Joe drove his wife away, away from him and the children they had created. She dealt with her pain by escaping. When she was not at work, she went to bingo at the local church. She took every opportunity to get out of the house, leaving the older kids to watch their younger sister. Her children were alone to deal with their father and his anger. They needed their mother to protect them from his verbal abuse, but they knew that she had to leave. They each built an emotional wall in an attempt to protect themselves from the harsh realities of their lives. Stress was a constant issue as they struggled to function in school. The teachers knew about the problems, but did nothing. They were allowed to fall through the cracks and minimal achievement was expected.

* * * * * *

In Joe's twisted reality, his wife's family interfered with their life and caused her to withhold the attention he deserved from her. Time did not lessen his jealous nature.

"Every time I turn around, someone from your family is at my front door. I know your sister was here today, eating my food and enjoying my house while I was at work."

Rummaging through the kitchen trash, searching for proof, he pulled out an empty can of tuna and the remnants of a pastry box.

"Did you have a feast today while you and your sister counseled each other about your problems? I don't want her knowing our business," he screamed, slamming the door on his way out to drown his sorrows.

Insecurity compelled him to eliminate the intruders. It didn't matter who was between them—her parents, her sisters, or even her children. The more he fought, the more he alienated his wife. Joe had a way of making typical families seem odd. He made fun of their traditions or routines, mocking family unity to make his dysfunctional family seem admirable through humor.

Buried deep beneath Joe's alcoholic behaviors and pain, a spark of creativity ignited into a flame. He had the talent to draw, paint, invent, and write poetry. He built the wildest projects out of items retrieved from other people's trash. His family was embarrassed when he went dumpster diving in the neighbor's garbage on trash day, but they marveled at the antiques he renovated.

"One man's garbage is another man's treasure," he would boast.

He made lamps out of old statues and tables with gold-painted bases out of discarded marble, all of which had an Italian flare. The pride he expressed was contagious, and his children basked in his joyful mood. But it was gone in a wink! Despite the happiness Joe felt during these moments, he still couldn't stop himself from fighting with Jean to get her attention. Most of the time, his children were in the way.

Anna tried to stay out of the house, but sometimes he caught her at home when Jean was out. Sitting in the dining room with his wine, Joe realized he wasn't alone in the house. His sixteen-year-old daughter was in her room. He walked to the front of the hall and shut off the switch that controlled the electricity for the second floor of the house. Listening to music as it blasted from the speakers in Anna's room, the record on her turntable let out a distorted whine as it came to a stop.

"Anna, come down here. I want to talk to you," Joe called from the hall.

Reluctantly, she walked down the stairs, avoiding eye contact with him, and took her seat at the dining room table. She could feel his squinting eyes on her. Anna knew what was coming and prayed it wouldn't take long.

"Your mother is no good!" His fiery eyes fixed on her face for any sign of sympathy. "She doesn't love me and she doesn't give me sex. All she wants is her family and her sister." He belted down another shot of scotch and searched for a reaction.

Expecting words of wisdom and getting nothing but silence, he became angry. Anna could feel him staring at her, but she resisted his intrusion as he interrogated her soul, seeking to convince her that he was right.

"Do you know that your mother won't have sex with me? She only loves her sister and her brother-in-law. She would crawl into bed with them if she could."

Anna silently averted his eyes, which she felt burning into her body. He waited for her to concede that her mother was no good and that he was the real victim. She knew that all she had to do was agree with him then he might let her leave. But all she could do was stare out the double glass sliding doors into the yard, fixing her eyes on the leaves in the trees or birds on the clothesline.

"Let me tell you something!" he said, as if he was about to give her knowledge. "Your mother doesn't care about you, either. She never took care of you kids." Anna felt guilty hearing the words that came out of his mouth, but she was helpless to defend her mother. He shook his head in disapproval and looked at his daughter with disgust. In his view, unless she had the ability to save him, she was useless.

* * * * * *

Frustrated by the daily commute, Joe's fingers clenched the wheel as he weaved in and out of traffic.

"Get off the road, you moron!" he yelled, flicking his cigarette out of the window with a bitter gesture. As he passed the slowly moving car in front of him, another took its place. He punched the steering wheel with so much anger that he bruised his hands, but he did not feel the pain. He hated the drive and the job at the other end of it, and began to think of a way out.

"I want to open a laundromat," he announced to his wife. "I'm going to quit my job and use my stock options to go into business."

Jean wasn't thrilled with the idea. They had almost ten thousand dollars in stock, and it was supposed to be security for the future. She knew he was not happy because the fights were getting more and more frequent. But maybe he will be happy and stop drinking, she thought to herself.

Jean gave her consent, even though she knew that she couldn't stop him anyway. Joe found a location a few towns away and bought secondhand washing machines and dryers. If the machines broke, he knew how to fix them to save money. Joe seemed happy and Jean was so busy with the kids that she didn't notice when things started going wrong. There were warning signs, but she was distracted and distant, not wanting to talk to him unless she had to. She kept her concerns to herself and her closest confidant, Lucia. Joe knew she was confiding to her family, which fueled their nightly fights.

He stopped bringing home money for the bills, telling Jean that the business was slow and they had to budget. Joe spent most of his time fixing the machines because they were constantly breaking down. In desperation, he convinced a friend who worked with him at Sears to become his partner. Now Joe had help but the profits were so slim that they couldn't keep it up. As the stress mounted, Joe started drinking during the day. He couldn't face his family, knowing that he could no longer provide for them.

Jean continued to cook dinner every night, and Joe noticed that there was plenty of food in spite of his meager earnings.

He grilled his wife, "Where did you get money for groceries?"

"My sister loaned me money. The kids were hungry and you haven't brought home a paycheck in weeks."

"I don't need your goddamn sister to support us," he screamed. "Tell her to keep her money."

Pride, resentment, and the pressure of trying to hold the business together worked on Joe until he cracked. He lost the laundromat and the money he invested, and once again took a job in the city, commuting to work every morning.

* * * * * *

As Joe tinkered under the hood of his truck, he watched a car roll slowly down the street. After the third time, it stopped in front of the house. Poor guy must be lost, Joe thought as he wiped his grease stained hands on a rag and walked toward the car. The man inside was crying.

"Can I help you?" Joe asked.

"Joey. It's me, your big brother."

Joe stared into the eyes of the man in the car. "Franc? Is that you?"

"How are you, Joey? I've been thinking about you."

"Park the car, Franc. Come on inside and have a cup of coffee."

When Jean saw the two of them walk into the kitchen, she nearly dropped the glass she was drying. "Franc! What a surprise."

"Hello, Jean. How have you been?"

Jean handed him a tissue, then realized that Joe had tears in his eyes too.

"I have to go pick up Linda, at school," she lied, leaving the two brothers alone to talk.

"Where's Dom? Why didn't he come with you?"

"I wanted him to, but he insisted that you should contact him since he is older."

"Does he know that you came to see me?"

"No, I didn't want to fight with him. Hey, maybe you could call him right now."

Joe began to tremble. He remembered the last time he tried to get in touch with Dom, and the pain was still fresh.

"What if he doesn't want to talk to me?" Joe sheepishly asked.

"Oh, he will," Franc assured him. "Here, I'll dial the number for you."

Franc waited until someone picked up on the other end, and then handed the phone to his little brother.

"Hello? Hello!" Dom's voice became annoyed at the silence.

"Hello, Dom! This is Joe."

"Joe? Joe who?"

"Joey, your brother," he replied, sorry now that he agreed to call.

"Joe! Is this really you? I'm so glad to hear your voice. We need to get together. It's been so long. I'll call Franc and set it up. We'll come to visit you and Jean in Long Island."

"What about next Sunday? You can all come over for dinner," Joe heard himself say, not considering that Jean would have to do the cooking and entertaining.

"Yeah. That would be great. We'll see you next weekend," Dom said.

Joe told Franc the plan. "Don't tell him that I came first," Franc begged.

Joe promised to keep the secret and walked his brother back to his car. He wasn't sure if he was up to having his brothers in his life again, but they were family, and he could not refuse.

When Jean came home, she was glad that the car was gone. "What did Franc want?"

"He wants to let bygones be bygones. He's coming back next week with Dom and their wives for dinner."

"They should cough up some of your father's money," Jean snapped, but she knew that Joe would never bring it up. "All right," she agreed. Jean was curious to find out about their lives, and thought it would be nice to see Tori again. Tori had always been nice to her.

Joe was happy that he was going to get together with his brothers, but all week he worried about what would happen after they met. He did not tell his sister about the dinner, and he felt guilty. "Maybe my brothers have changed over the years," Joe hoped. But in his heart, he knew that even though things started off well, their true natures would eventually surface and the family would be at each other's throats once more.

The next Sunday, the brothers stared at each other across the table as their wives made small talk. They agreed that it was good to put the whole mess behind them.

"What about Dolly?" Joe asked.

"There's no way I'm going to talk to that bitch," Dom yelled.

Hearing those words, Joe decided he did not want to get sucked back into the family turmoil. He was happy his brothers were no longer mad at him and, as they left, he promised that he would stay in touch. But he never saw either one of them again.

Janet Sierzant

Each Day of Our Lives

Our days are guided
By the Lord in his way
We pray to awake each morning
To be blessed by one more day

All of our joys and sorrows
Are issued by his command
And to all this day and its destiny
He holds in his loving hand

Given by him another new day
And all of its many hours
With its joy or tears or misfortune
Every moment is controlled by his powers

So fear not of any evil
That is set before thee
For by our love for him
He will surely set you free

The Lord will forgive us
As he has done many times before
By our love and faith in him
He will open each and every door

So we ask him his forgiveness
If we should wrong our fellow man
For in his caring love from him
He will surely understand

And as our day closes we pray
The Lord will awaken us
With one more happy day

— Gemini Joe

Chapter Fifteen

Joe was proud of his Italian heritage. He would say, "The Romans have given more to humanity than any other ethnic group. I defy anyone to show me different. Of course, we had some bad elements in there, but you take the good with the bad. Look at all the famous painters, poets and architects that came from Italy. We are a creative people, and no one can deny that!"

As a child, Anna would wake up to pages of cartoon drawings that he left for her to find on the coffee table. She couldn't believe that her father produced these wonders, and she welled up with pride. Anna protected her image of him by using the good to bury the bad parts of his personality. His anger was scary but when he was in a good mood, Anna basked in his attention, which could end abruptly if she said the wrong thing. His praise was like candy: a sweetness that didn't last long, but always left her wanting more. Her father's creativity somehow gave her what she needed from him—a connection. If she had a school assignment, he would excitedly offer to help, and Anna received his full attention. Fear and excitement washed over Anna when he noticed her. But the slightest wrong move could turn him into a monster with his disproving stares. Anna let him take over her projects, unable to object to his creative ideas.

When Anna was in fifth grade, he built a covered wagon that was the envy of her classmates. The teacher surely knew that Anna didn't make it, but she kept it anyway and displayed it in the glass case of the school hallway.

In sixth grade, he built a space project. As she carried it to her classroom, the other kids followed, laughing. "It's nothing but a box with a hole."

Anna tried to ignore them as she set it on the teacher's desk and plugged the cord into the wall outlet. All her classmates crowded around to figure it out what it was. When they peeked inside, a galaxy came alive before their eyes. A small light inside a flying saucer that hung from a string illuminated florescent stars and drawings of planets and comets, shooting across a background of black construction paper.

"How did you make this?" they all asked.

Anna suppressed her guilt as the other students admired the work of art. She felt like a fraud, but she kept the secret. Her father always waited for her at the end of the school day, as excited as a small boy on Christmas. He wanted Anna to tell him how everyone loved it, again and again and again.

* * * * * *

Jean waited anxiously for her husband to come home. She held tightly to the letter that arrived for him, hopeful that their life was going to change. She recalled how she helped him pick the right clothes and arranged his paperwork for the presentation to the board of the toothpaste company. For once, one of Joe's ideas was about to become a reality. His design for a toothpaste tube with an attached cap was going to make them rich.

Even at the tender age of fourteen, Joe had a knack of looking at something mechanical and thinking of a better way. He noticed that no matter how hard he tried to skate fast, something held him back. Examining the bottom of his skate, he found that the manufacturer place a rubber block to slow the wheels down. Of course, the safety of small children had motivated them to deter the speed of their product, but Joe did not see the necessity and began to disassemble wheels and remove the block.

"I'm going to go as fast as the wind," he said, with a sly smile on his face.

Once he reattached the wheels, he used his key to adjust each skate, careful to make them as tight as possible. Loose skates had a way of shifting off your foot and landing alongside your ankle as you hit the dirt or the cement. Joe had many scars from skating. He knew that he was taking a risk, but wouldn't his friends be green with envy as he whizzed by, leaving them behind and bewildered. He skated over to call for Jimmy. The other guys were already in the park, but Joey wanted to make sure his best friend witnessed his victory.

"Wow, look at him go," the other boys yelled. "How did you do that?" They begged to know as he flew past them in every race. Joe smiled as he passed them, watching the expressions of amazement. When he had his fill, he benevolently agreed to fix their skates too. Joe basked in their admiration as they looked to him for his help.

Joe had a way of looking at things. Ideas for new inventions came to him all the time. He was always looking to improve a design or create something that would make life easier. Using his drawing ability, he sketched out a prototype.

"You need to get that patented," wise people instructed him.

He should have taken their advice. Instead, he listened to the easy way out.

"All you need to do is mail it to yourself, certified. But don't open the envelope. Your idea will be safe and no one will be able to steal it."

Joe continued to document each new idea that came to him, and then mailed it to himself. While working at the auto garage, he thought of a better way to change the lug nuts to change all five at once instead of one at a time. As a mechanic for Sears, he thought of a way to adjust the legs of heavy appliances. Even around the house, Joe thought of innovations to make life easier. "Wouldn't it be great if you could just dial the amount of coffee that you need instead of having to scoop it out all the time?" he asked his wife.

His proudest moment came out of frustration. "What's wrong with you kids," he yelled. "Why can't you put the cap back on the toothpaste when you are finished?" Joe looked down at the tube in disgust. Hair and dirt was stuck to the opening, and the cap was nowhere to be found. "What do I have to do? Glue the cap to the tube?"

It was morning, and his mind was not yet clouded with alcohol. A spark ignited as he ran to the garage with the tube of toothpaste. He emerged with a design. Joe mailed it to himself certified, then sent it out to toothpaste manufacturers, hoping someone would like his idea. Someone did, and he was invited to present his prototype to the company board.

In his usual, cocky manner, he strode into the office where a dozen suited men sat around a table. He knew his idea was great and he enjoyed being the center of attention. He watched as their eyes widened and their heads nodded affirmatively. With a big smile, the CEO assured Joe that they would get back to him soon.

A few weeks later, a response to Joe's invention was in the mailbox. Jean jumped up when she heard his truck roll up the driveway. Before he could enter the front door, she was jumping up and down, waving the letter.

"We're going to be rich," she squealed with delight. "Hurry up! Open it!"

Joe smiled as he tore it open. At last, things were going his way. Jean watched his face as he read the one-page letter.

"What's wrong?" she said, as his smile disappeared.

"They're not interested," he growled, tossing the paper in the trash.

Jean retrieved the letter after Joe had stormed out and driven himself to the bar. She cried herself to sleep that night and did not hear Joe come in.

* * * * * *

When Joe could not get the attention he wanted at home, he usually found it at the bar or with his friends at the Sons of Italy Club, an organization formed with the sole purpose of preserving the culture of Italian Americans. Members were mostly Italian, but a few were Jewish, Irish and German with active spouses in the club. The Mafia was not acknowledged within the Sons of Italy, but everyone knew who its members were. They retained their power by staying undercover and frowned on people like John Gotti, who wore expensive suits and flaunted his activities. This kind of attention was dangerous and put everyone at risk. As far as the Sons of Italy were concerned, there was no Mafia! Instead, they gravitated toward politics, discovering that the power achieved through legal channels could be just as valuable, if not more.

Joe sat drinking at the local bar when one of his friends from the club sat down on the stool next to him. Joe had already been there a couple of hours, and was sitting with his head in his hands.

"Hey, Joe!" Lou said, slapping him on the back. "What's up with you?"

Intoxicated, Joe began complaining about his life.

"I spend most of my time working and no one appreciates it," he whined. "The commute is killing me, and I have nothing to show for it."

"Why don't you get a job on the Island?" Lou asked.

"I wish that I could, but I don't know of any jobs," Joe slurred.

"Joe, you need to get into the political scene here on Long Island if you want a local job."

Joe remembered that his neighbor, Al, mentioned something about joining the Republican Club when he first moved onto the block. He recalled his neighbor's words through the haze of alcohol.

"New York is a democratic state, but in this town, everyone is Republican," Al warned. "You need to come to one of the meetings with me Joe. I think you would find it very interesting."

Joe wasted no time. The next day, he paid Al a visit.

"When is the next Republican Club meeting? I would like to go."

Joe's neighbor smiled. After four months of trying to convince Joe to join the club, he was now standing at his front door.

"It's about time that you came to your senses, Joe."

Al agreed to take Joe along to the meeting that week. Joe nervously walked into the rented space above a local store that was used for their meetings. Men dressed in stylish Italian suits stood talking in groups. Joe felt very important as his neighbor took him around the room, introducing him to the most influential men in town. His charismatic personality kicked into high gear as he lobbied to be included and accepted into the inner circle.

"I like this guy," they said among themselves. Lou was right, Joe thought. Joining the Republican Club opened doors.

The meeting came to order. Joe was impressed as they discussed the upcoming election.

"We cannot leave the election to chance," the committee chairman began. "Nixon must be elected, and it is up to us to make that happen."

He ended the speech by reminding everyone, "Now, Get the Machine Out," which was a code phrase for the plan to put a Republican in office.

"I'll see what I can do to get you a county job, but you need to become a committeeman, Joe," Al whispered after the meeting. Committee men volunteered to go door to door, convincing democratic voters to stand with them for Nixon.

Joe did just that and began spending less time at the bar. He used the computer-generated list supplied to him by the club to target past democratic voters in his town, knocking on their doors. When the first door slammed shut, Joe was discouraged. He was not good with rejection of any kind, and now he was a putting himself in the line of fire. What would his father have done? The neurons in Joe's brain began to fire at a faster pace. The next time he knocked on a door, he was prepared.

The old man looked at him from behind suspicious eyes.

"What do you want?"

"My name is Joe and I am a delegate for the Republican Party," Joe began.

"I'm a Democrat," the man sneered, beginning to close the door.

"I just want to find out if you have any grievances that I can help with," Joe quickly responded. He pulled out a small black book and a pen, ready to write down the man's complaints.

The old man stared at him for a moment.

"Can you do something about that pot hole down the street? It's ruining my car. I called five times and no one will come out to fix it."

"I'll see what I can do," Joe promised as he wrote down the man's address and complaint. He promised to resolve their issues, even though his words entered skeptical ears.

"If you could do this, I'll vote for whoever you want me to," they claimed.

Joe continued, feeling clever. In one day, he filled his book with promises and impatiently waited for the next club meeting to present it to the people in charge. Joe was finally being noticed. Everyone was impressed and buzzed around him like bees.

"Joe, baby, this is great! If we get some of these grievances fixed, there is a good chance they will vote with us!"

At the Republican election headquarters, phone calls were made, and methodically they went about solving the problems, one by one. Joe returned to the potential voters, announcing that their problems were being solved. He loved bringing good news and receiving the admiration people showered on him. In return, they made good on their promise to vote republican in the next election, which helped Richard Nixon win by a landslide in the presidential election while Nelson Rockefeller was elected governor of New York.

* * * * * *

The Republican Party grew on Long Island, and things began to change. The leading Italian republicans took on positions such as judges, county managers and heads of state. The Sons of Italy was the instrument that ignited the grassroots growth of the Republican Party in New York. In their meetings, the Sons of Italy used code words to discuss political views and plans. And Joe was in the thick of it. The political machine was churning on Long Island and Joe was eager to participate in the process. His career was on the upswing, and there was no stopping him. He had friends in high places, and everyone loved his upbeat personality. His presence at fundraising dinners and social events cemented the nickname given to him years before: Gemini Joe.

With the election of a republican president, three republicans and one democrat would be entitled to government management jobs in any particular area. As a prominent committeeman for the Republican Club, Joe became politically active in the town. His new friends kept their promise: they gave him a county job, and he found himself on the road to a new career.

Joe's new job was to beautify the local beaches. The first beach was Florence Beach, and Joe took it as a good omen. He knew someone above was looking out for him as he renovated the beach with the same name as his mother. His perfectionist nature and creative mind transformed the small, polluted beach into a place enjoyed by families and children. Trash was drudged out of the ocean and machines filtered the sand. He requested money to add a grassy area with picnic tables and a playground for the children. His efforts brought him recognition from the county as the mayor honored him with awards and his picture appeared in the paper.

Janet Sierzant

Butterfly

Poor little caterpillar climbing up a tree,
Wishing every day to be pretty as can be
The world thought her ugly, the world called her slow
But her faith in God gave her the courage to go
For in her heart was a secret that only God did know

She had something special and fine
To this lowly creature, God would be kind
Shelter to sleep the hurts away
Until there come a better day

A heart humble and bold,
acceptance of challenges untold

One day in spring, under a sky of gold
Her beauty had begun to unfold

Away she flew, with pride in flight
Leaving behind all memories of despair and fright
To this creature as with all God's beings
She was given the gift to live out her dreams

— Gemini Joe

Chapter Sixteen

It didn't take long for Joe to be promoted to a county supervising job and assigned to maintain all buildings in the parks department. He worked without supervision, coming and going as he pleased in a county-assigned vehicle. Sometimes he went home to spy on his wife. As he pulled up in front of his house, he saw his sister-in-law's car. Silent as a stone, he walked in to see them eating and laughing around his kitchen table. He left unnoticed, with a bitter taste in his mouth, but it always provided an excuse to fight with his wife after dinner and disappear into the night, slamming the front door behind him. Even the neighbors knew his destination. They would see Joe sneaking in and out of his garage as they congregated in front of their houses in their lawn chairs. He entered the garage in his work clothes and emerged dressed to the hilt. They nicknamed him Dean Martin because they often observed him staggering back into the garage late at night.

"There he goes again," they would say, feeling sympathy for his wife.

Drinking Man's Lament

I led myself to drink
To face each trying day
I made myself to think
I could drown my troubles away

I found out from my hurts within
That all my troubles learned to swim
It was true, without a doubt
The drink I could not do without

Drink prolongs beginnings
And rushes in all ends
So pass the word my drinking friends
The truth your mind will bend

— Gemini Joe

The county job paid well and offered good benefits, but it had its downside for Jean. She was required to show up on her husband's arm at all the political events. She loved to socialize, but knew she would have to pay for her enjoyment at the end of each night when her husband drunkenly interrogated her about who she spoke to, accusing her of flirting and making a fool out of him.

"Keep an eye on your wife," his boss kidded him. "You may lose her to Johnny over there."

Like gasoline on a hot fire, the words fueled Joe's jealousy and he looked at his wife as the perpetrator. "You're making me look bad, you cocksucker," he whispered into her ear.

Jean knew that the ride home was going to be bad and she wasn't going to get much sleep that night. For awhile, Jean refused to go to the dinners and dances, hoping to avoid an inevitable fight, but that only caused another fight. Joe did not want to go alone and found himself at the bar instead.

"Let me tell you something, you motherfucker. You are going to pay for this. I have a surprise in store for you," he threatened.

Jean's only escape was to go out with her girlfriends. She went to bingo at the church every Tuesday and Thursday, and played cards every Friday night at one of the girl's houses. Joe suspected that she was going out with other men and often followed her before he went drinking at the bar.

When Jean escaped the house to visit with her friends, she saw her husband's car in her rearview mirror. Ignoring it became easy since it was a daily occurrence, and Jean anxiously proceeded to her destination, where she would be out of his range. Every Friday evening, the girls met at each other's houses to play cards — everyone's except Jean's. They piled their coats onto the hostess's bed and take their places around the dining room table. The hostess would impress her friends with the appetizers and snacks she cooked. Jean could relax and be herself, laughing and talking as if she hadn't a care in the world. But as she drove home, the reality of her life became heavier with every block closer to her house, and she felt her mood descend. Joe waited for her at the kitchen table with his bottle of scotch.

"What are these gray hairs all over your coat?" he accused one night.

"Its fur from my girlfriend's coat," she said in a tone that indicated he was out of his mind.

"I don't believe you," Joe yelled. "I think it is hair from your lover. You can't fool me. I know you're seeing someone. If I catch you, I'll bury you." Joe's suspicion took over all logic and reason. He came home every day on his lunch break to try and catch his wife in a compromising position.

"I know you are seeing someone," he said, completely satisfied with himself for discovering a card in her car that his daughter forgot to take with her. "Who is Nicky?" he demanded.

"I don't know what you're talking about," Jean angrily replied. "Leave me alone." She tried not to show fear, but she was afraid and had good reason to be.

* * * * * *

Jean frowned when she opened the invitation that came in the mail. She loved weddings, but it was the perfect setting for her husband to make a scene. But since this wedding was for Joe's sister's daughter, there was no getting around it.

Joe walked straight to the open bar at the reception hall. He had a head start before the wedding ceremony, but he couldn't consume enough alcohol. He stumbled to the designated table where Dolly was sitting with Tony and Jean.

"Wasn't my daughter the most beautiful bride ever?" Dolly asked.

"Yeah sure," Joe slurred. His eyes fixed on his wife and he didn't try to hide his disgust for her. "You're a cunt," he snarled.

"Joe, don't talk to your wife that way," his sister scolded.

"What do you care?"

"Don't make a scene, Joe. This is my daughter's wedding and there are a lot of people."

"Yeah, right! Everyone except our family! We should have three tables, but you were too stubborn to invite your brothers, Frank and Dom, their wives and all your nieces."

"Joe, you know that they wouldn't have come."

"Let me tell you something. That's what is wrong with our family. Everyone would rather fight like a son of a bitch than to stick together. Mom must be spinning in her grave to know that all her sacrifice was for nothing."

"Joe, please lower your voice," Tony pleaded.

"Jean, maybe you should take him home," Dolly urged.

"I'm not going anywhere with this bitch. I'm going to get another drink. Does anyone else want one?"

As Joe turned away from the bar with his scotch, he found himself face to face with his nephew, Anthony, who towered above him. He was at least two feet taller than Joe and twice his weight in muscle.

"Come on, Uncle Joe. I'm taking you home."

"I don't want to leave," he protested as Anthony led him out by his arm.

Anthony shoved his uncle out of the reception hall and toward his car. Joe could not stand straight as he cursed and argued. He was stopped in his tracks when he felt his nephew's hands around his neck.

"You son of a bitch! You had to ruin my sister's wedding didn't you? Shut up and get in the car," Anthony yelled, keeping his left hand on Joe's throat while opening the car door with his right.

Unable to breathe, Joe panicked, looking to people passing on the street for help. But no one stopped. They just kept walking, not wanting to get in the middle of a bad situation. Joe passed out in the back seat and woke up on his sister's sofa. He did not know what happened to make his nephew so mad.

Later when Joe called his sister, Anthony answered the phone.

"Hey, Anthony! You almost killed me at the wedding," he jokingly said.

"Yeah," his nephew laughed. "I should have squeezed a little harder." Then he hung up.

Joe stared at the receiver, confused and upset that someone could hate him that much.

* * * * * *

Increasingly irrational, Joe used alcohol to numb his brain. His inability to cope with his job became harder to hide. People were starting to talk. Suspecting that he was going to the bar every afternoon, his boss ordered someone to follow him. He wasn't at the bar, but his truck was parked in front of his house every day for hours and did not return until it was time to clock out. One afternoon, there was a knock on the door.

"Tony, Bobby, what are you guys doing here?" Joe asked.

"Joe, I'm sorry! We're here to get the truck," Tony said, taking a step back.

"What? Why? Who sent you?" Joe sobered up enough to know he was in big trouble.

"The boss wants to see you in his office tomorrow morning but right now, Joe, I need the keys."

Joe went into the kitchen and returned with the keys to the truck. As he removed them from his key ring, he said to his two co-workers, "There must be a mistake. I'll talk to Angelo tomorrow."

When they left, he sat down at the kitchen table to finish off his bottle of scotch before passing out in the chair.

The next day he drove his own car over to the office and walked in, acting as if nothing was wrong. He walked into his boss's office. Angelo sat behind his desk puffing on a cigar. From the minute Joe joined the Republican Club, Angelo had been his mentor. Friends in high places always helped Joe get ahead.

"Joe, I have a problem," Angelo said as he stubbed out his cigar. "I am told you've been drinking on the job, and I hear you've been using the county truck for personal use."

"Angelo, I would never drink on the job. Sometimes I go home for lunch. That's why the truck was at my house. I can't lose this job. I have a wife and four kids." Someone snitched, he thought to himself, no longer listening to his boss. Angelo's cigar continued to smoke in the ashtray, which streamed into Joe's eyes.

"Joe, Joe, do you hear me? Are you all right? You are my friend, and I don't want to fire you."

"Angelo, I don't know what you heard, but it isn't true. You know me! Why would I do anything to destroy your trust?"

"I know, Joe, but its 1973, and things are changing politically. I have to protect myself. I have two kids in college and my wife spends money like water."

"They can't do anything without you, Angelo. You're the best thing that has ever happen to this county," Joe groveled. "I defy anyone to go against you."

"Joe, you put me in a delicate position, but I'm going to give you another chance. I'm going to have to reassign you, though. It wouldn't look right if you keep the same job. I want you to report to the Parks Department in Mineola tomorrow. Tell them Angelo sent you for the maintenance supervisor position. You won't have a vehicle, but you will keep your job in the county. I'm giving you one more chance, Joe. Don't let me down."

Joe left his Angelo's office to drown his sorrows, bemoaning his life and the tragedy of his career that was once so promising.

* * * * * *

When Joe arrived at the department headquarters in Minneola, he took the elevator to the Parks Department office. He felt optimistic because Angelo was on his side, and everyone would know that he had clout—everyone except the employees in Mineola. They did not seem impressed with Joe's credentials.

"Take a seat over there and fill out this application," instructed a heavy-set woman wearing too much make-up.

Joe looked down at the clipboard. Boy! This is new, he thought. Joe was never required to go through the formalities before. A handshake was always enough.

After returning the application to the receptionist, Joe waited to meet his new boss. His hands began to shake as he resisted the urge to leave and head to the bar. After forty-five minutes, he stood up, disgusted and fed up. Before he closed the door, he heard someone call his name.

"Joe Fuccino? Hi, I'm Mr. Benedetto. Come on into my office so we can talk."

Joe followed the tall lanky man dressed in a starched suit. He looked very formal and business-like and Joe began to feel uncomfortable in his blue county uniform.

"I hear that Angelo from Oyster Bay recommended you for this job. You would be in charge of the building maintenance for this building. I have looked over your application and it seems like you are well qualified for the job. You can start tomorrow."

"Yeah, Angelo and I go way back. I am very involved in the Republican Club."

Mr. Benedetto stared blankly at Joe. "That's nice," he said distractedly. He rose and shook Joe's hand, guiding him toward the door. "If you have any problems, come to me," he said, closing the door abruptly.

Joe left the building feeling disorientated. What was that? he wondered, heading for the bar. The Republican Party's credibility declined with the ongoing investigation of Nixon's presidency. It was no longer prestigious to be in the club, but Joe did not care. He just wanted to stay in the county job long enough to collect his pension. Early retirement was always one of the perks for working a government job. He knew that he could make more money doing side jobs, repairing machines and cars. Besides, money from side jobs was easier to hide from his wife.

"Why should I fork over all my hard-earned money to that bitch. She'll only gamble it away at bingo," he rationalized. He did not return home until the bar closed, then tried to catch a few hours of sleep.

The next morning, Joe found himself in the boiler room at the bottom floor of the building. He hated it. It was hot and stifling with flickering fluorescent lights.

I'm truly in hell, he thought. One of his jobs was to ensure the pressure did not rise higher than the optimal level in the boiler. Alone in the boiler room with no one around to watch, Joe numbed his mind with the bottle he hid in the back of the filing cabinet. Oblivious to the rising temperature, he cried about his life at his desk in the corner. Unnoticed, the pressure in the boiler increased until it exploded, propelling Joe upwards. Shaken and bruised, he opened his eyes to the onlookers.

"Joe, are you all right? Stay still. An ambulance is on the way."

But Joe did not feel anything. He closed his eyes again during his ride to the hospital, not caring what happened to him. He escaped with a few bruises and no broken bones. An investigation showed nothing unusual. A faulty switch took the blame and he was soon back to work. Joe walked away yet again from the consequences of his drinking.

Everyone sensed his drinking problem and tried to put distance between them. He knew it, and blamed his wife for his problems. "I could've gone far in this town if I had a good wife," he yelled.

* * * * * *

Years of fighting and turmoil followed until it became a natural state of family life. Joe alienated everyone around him, with no one escaping his accusations. Disappointment was clear in his eyes as he squinted at his children and asked,

"What's wrong with you?" His words flushed their self-esteem down the nearest toilet. They should have been carefree in their innocence. Instead, they functioned in a fog, never knowing when their world was going to explode. When they kept their distance from him, Joe tried to make his children feel guilty.

"You don't care about me," he would whisper. "I don't get any love."

"I love you, Dad," Anna replied, trying to convince him.

"No, you don't!" he would answer, leaving her to wonder if she really didn't. "Just grow up and get out."

Tension grew as Joe's children grew up and started to voice their opinions. During his rare appearances at home, he was insulting and degrading, calling them Retard Numbers One, Two, and Three. Still a baby, his youngest daughter was spared the label.

There was no talk of what they wanted to be when they grew up. He doused any spark of interest to further education. "You're not college material," he said, crushing dreams and the slightest belief that they could be "normal."

Since college was out of the question, marriage was the only option for his daughters, and Anna accepted the first proposal that came her way. George was jealous and possessive, but as the wedding day drew closer, Anna ignored her mother's warnings about him. Jean begged her to call it off, but Joe kept his opinions to himself. After a big wedding, where Joe enjoyed the spotlight of the bride's father, Anna realized that her new husband, George, was just like her father.

"Why did it take you so long? Who did you see at the supermarket? Who did you talk to?" George asked suspiciously.

After a couple of months of marriage, Anna began to loss weight. She smoked one cigarette after another and played solitaire to distract from her unhappiness. One night, she returned from a family bridal shower to find George drunk and ready for a fight. When he pushed her, she snapped. The only one she could think of to call for help was her father. She ran to the phone.

"Dad, I need you," were the only words she had to say before he was at her door helping to collect her belongings.

"I never liked him," Joe said. "Be careful if he comes around and asks you to come out and talk to him. He'll try to talk you into giving him another chance." Joe knew all the tricks!

Anna found herself back in the home she had tried to escape, but now that she had a taste of the outside world, she became even more restless. She wanted to have her own home, but for now, she needed a job. When her uncle agreed to sponsor her for a clerical job in his government-based corporation, Anna jumped at the opportunity. It didn't take long for her to forget about a domestic life as she excelled in her new career.

The electrical department was on one side of her office and the mechanical department was on the other. Anna spotted a good looking boy at a workbench in the mechanical section. Her heart began to beat faster every time she passed him. She finally mustered the courage to say hello. He looked up from his work and smiled. His eyes twinkled and she melted under his gaze. Their first date was magical and Anna fell instantly in love. As she ascended to new heights of emotion, she began to exhibit the traits of her father and it scared her. Obsessed with her heart's desire and the hope of becoming his wife, she sucked the air out of a room, demanding love in return. The more she pushed the more he pulled, until all she achieved was to drive him away. Anna was devastated as she tried to figure out what went wrong. She asked herself if mutual love was even possible or if the person who loved the other more was always at a disadvantage.

"A man has to love you more," her mother lectured.

Maybe she was right, but it sure felt good to love someone with all her heart. Still, the pain of not being loved back was too much for Anna to bear. If being in love made her jealous and possessive like her father, she knew that she was better off without it.

* * * * * *

At eighteen, Joe's only son began to butt heads with his father. When he forgot to take out the trash, Joey woke up in a pile of trash.

"That will teach you to forget trash day," his father slurred with a smug, drunken grin. After almost coming to blows with his father, Joey decided to move to Houston, Texas, with his friends to work in construction, building houses. He wrote home about blue skies and clouds that hung so low, he could almost touch them.

Anna envied his escape. But she was soon rescued by an old acquaintance that appeared on her doorstep from out of the blue. Anna knew Dan from the neighborhood. He was funny and made her laugh. Although Anna insisted that they could only be friends, he stubbornly persisted until she gave in. He loved to travel and camp in the woods, and it was the escape to nature that made her feel safe. She married him and moved into his father's house until they could find a place of their own. When Anna found out that she was expecting a baby, she feared that they might have to take her parents up on their offer to occupy the basement apartment. Then a letter came from her brother in Texas that changed her life and, although she didn't know it at the time, the lives of her parents too.

"Come on down," Joey wrote. "They're building houses like crazy here. I could get your husband a job."

When Anna announced that they were moving, Jean was devastated. She was losing her children and there was nothing she could do to stop it. Her heart was broken as she watched Anna leave Long Island with all her earthly possessions and her future grandchild. Things would never be the same for Jean. As her children left the house one by one, she sunk into a depression.

* * * * *

Jean was left alone in the house with her youngest child, Linda, trying to cope with her life. She stopped taking care of herself and spent all her time watching television in the small room they called a den. As their marriage crumbled, decisions had to be made.

"Maybe we should move to Pennsylvania," she suggested to Joe.

Jean had convinced him to buy the land a few years earlier, when a friend told her about it at bingo. They drove up one weekend and decided to take a loan, hoping that it would be paid off by the time they retired.

Joe flat out refused. "I'm not leaving my house and working up there."

"We could build a new house on our land," his wife pleaded. "Maybe we would be happier in the mountains."

"No" he repeated. "I can't leave my job."

"You could put in for early retirement," she tried once more.

He started to soften. It was tempting to think he could leave the pressures of his job behind. He wasn't happy with the way his career turned out and he was getting tired of this town.

"I'll think about it," he told her before he left for the bar. Jean knew that she had planted the seed and gave the idea room to bloom. Joe wanted to escape the life that once held so much promise for his future. He felt the eyes of the town upon him and could not hold his head up anymore. Maybe we could start a new life, he thought. And it didn't hurt to know that there would be more distance between his wife and her family.

Joe agreed to sell the house and called a real estate broker. The agent listened as Joe described his troubles and his reasons for selling.

"You may have to bring the price down," the broker baited.

"Do what you have to do to sell it," Joe told her.

The three-story colonial house never went on the market. They hoped to sell the house by spring, but the agent showed it only one time—to her son. The house was sold, and they had to leave sooner than they expected. Joe put in for early retirement in the county. His pension was enough to cover most of their expenses, and the sale of the house brought a nice profit. Joe knew that he could get handyman jobs off the books and looked forward to an easier life. Eligibility for retirement would come in the spring, but that was four months away. In exchange for his handyman skills, he was offered a room from a woman he knew from the bar.

On a windy fall day, Jean left for Pennsylvania with her fourteen-year-old daughter to wait for her husband to tie up the loose ends.

Janet Sierzant

Cold and Lonely Night

*I sit alone in this dwelling
That once I called my home
The night seems long and lonely
In every room I roam*

*In this house were voices
Of laughter and of tears
But now there is just silence
And loneliness and fears*

*Dreaming of a chance
To somehow turn back time
I sit and think all through the night
In loneliness of mine*

*In morning light I'll leave
The kingdom-home I've know
Afraid to face the future
And the great unknown*

— Gemini Joe

Jean and Linda drove over the Throgs Neck and George Washington bridges to leave New York. Slipping and sliding all over the icy roads, Jean kept both white-knuckled hands on the wheel. The windshield wipers left streaks on the frosted glass and it was hard to see through the blizzard conditions. By some kind of miracle, they made it to Pennsylvania.

"How did you drive with these bald tires?" a gas station attendant asked in horror. "You could have been killed."

Jean held back her tears when she realized that her husband did not check the car before they left and probably didn't care if they broke down on the road.

Jean and Linda settled into a rental house until they could build their own home. Linda was excited to start her new school, but she wondered when her father would arrive. Jean waited for Joe who claimed to have things to take care of on Long Island.

Snowed in their house for weeks, the wind whistled as it searched for a way to get in. Joe had promised to come before the storm, but he never showed up. Fear that he may have had an accident quickly changed to anger when Jean discovered that he was fine.

"I had some things to do. Are you sure that you want to live up there?"

He seemed to be changing his mind about moving and Jean began to sense that something was wrong. She called her sister Lucia for advice.

"I'm scared, Lucia. I feel so isolated up here and I'm not sure what Joe is doing."

"Has he called?"

"No, but I don't think he plans to move up here."

"What makes you think that?"

"He's not sending the money to start construction."

"That money is sitting in the bank," Lucia warned." He could take it all."

"Maybe I should go back to Long Island," Jean decided even before the words passed her lips.

"Tell him to find another house before he gets any ideas," Lucia urgently counseled.

Jean wasted no time and convinced Joe to buy another house on the Island. They returned to a different house, but things went back to the way they had always been. Joe found himself in a different town with different bars and different people. Gemini Joe found a new audience to entertain. The relationship between him and his wife did not change when they moved into the new house. The attachment he felt for his old house was gone and he did not have memories to tie him to the new house. Time was lost and wasted, and there was no going back. So he forged ahead with new friends, playing the lead role of victim, needing to be the center of attention. He wasn't happy until everyone knew he felt unloved. He sought the advice of strangers as he told his side of the story.

* * * * * *

Ann was not an attractive woman. She was tall and lanky with black hair that she swept up in a bun. Her black eyes divulged confidence, announced her opinions and took control. She was not the kind of woman that could tolerate Joe's constant complaining. Robust in statue, she did not have many feminine qualities, but her fierce determination made her a force to be reckoned with. As a single mother caring for her retarded son, she fought for what she needed to survive and rented out rooms in her house for extra cash. Ann had gusto for life and laughed at the slightest inclination. As a bartender's assistant, she was privy to her clients' life stories, especially after a few drinks.

"If your wife doesn't love you what are you doing there?" she asked Joe.

Joe thought she made sense and fed off her confidence. He knew Ann for little over a year. At first, she poured empathy along with his scotch, but he could tell that she was starting to get a little annoyed with him lately.

"Do you really think I should leave?" he asked.

"What do you have to lose? You could stay with me," Ann said. "You're in luck! One of my tenants just left and there is an empty room. You could live with me if you agree to do some maintenance around the house."

Joe stared at the woman behind the bar. Maybe she is my route of escape, he thought. Ann was a strong woman who could guide him into a new future. She could protect him from falling through the cracks.

Jean was accustomed to her husband staying out all night and stopped keeping track of him. The only day that was important to her was payday. His pension check came regularly and she depended on it to pay bills. When he didn't come home with his pension check, she began to worry. Days went by and there was no sign of him. She thought of going to look for him at the bars, but stubbornly decided that she would not stoop to that level. But she surprised him one day, catching him in the house when he thought she wasn't home.

"Where's the money? You haven't given me money to buy food," she said.

He quickly gathered some clothes and promised to bring her some money from the bank, but Jean knew he wasn't coming back. For months she had sensed that there was another woman, but never thought he would have the nerve to leave Jean and their daughter.

A few days later, Jean received a phone call from her sister-in-law, Tori, informing that Dom had been diagnosed with cancer.

"They opened him up and he was full," she sobbed into the phone. "The doctors stitched him back up and sent him home. There's nothing they can do for him. We don't know how long he can hang on, but he is asking to see Joe."

"I'm sorry, but he moved out. I will try to find him and let him know," Jean promised. But Joe seemed to have disappeared. She suspected that he was living with a woman from the bar, but refused to go there asking for him. Dom died within the week. Joe was not at his funeral.

One week turned into two, then three, until she had no other choice. Finally, she filed a petition in the family court to force her husband for support. Before long, the sheriff was at Jean's door, serving her with the blue legal papers of the divorce. Safely watching from his car, Joe saw as his wife was served the papers. He waited after the door closed, giving her enough time to absorb the news. Then he walked through the front door to find Jean sobbing at the dining room table.

"Don't do this now," Jean begged. She was not happy with Joe, but feared the prospect of being on her own after all these years. The situation developed slowly and became tolerable to her over time. Like a frog that does not sense the danger of its changing surroundings, Jean had waited until it was too late.

"Please wait until Linda graduates high school," she begged.

"It's over," Joe smirked. "I can't wait to be free of you."

"You're going to die alone," Jean predicted through bitter tears. She did not realize that this was the greatest gift Joe ever gave her. She would have been a martyr for the rest of her live if he did not initiate the break.

Once Joe began the divorce proceedings, there was no turning back. News of their divorce blindsided Anna and her brother, but Dana and Linda were devastated. They all were accustomed to their parents war dance, but accepted the relationship as part of their normal family life.

Janet Sierzant

Who is to Blame

I found myself asleep one day, because I felt a pain
Maybe I just dreamed it all, and I'm the one to blame

I could not rest or let it be, perhaps it really was all me
If it's true, I feel so small; will I rise above it all

I searched my mind and all my wit
Then tried to make the best of it

— Gemini Joe

Chapter Seventeen

Jean was confident that she would come out on top in the divorce proceedings, winning her house and a decent amount of alimony and child support. After all, Joe abandoned her and his youngest daughter. But the court proceedings were ugly, and she soon realized she didn't have a chance. After so many years of working for the county, Joe knew all the right people and his book of favors was thick. As they filed into the courtroom, county officials smiled and greeted him by name.

"Hey, Joe, how's it going?"

"Joey, baby, where've you been? I haven't seen you at the club lately."

"Aye! Gemini! Lets get together Friday night and I'll buy you a drink."

Doom washed over Jean as she sat on a bench with her lawyer. "It's not going to be easy," he warned Jean.

It wasn't. Joe was ready for a fight. He had bugged their home phone, which he found out was not illegal as long as his name was on the phone bill. Listening from the device he set up in the garage, he heard his wife and sister-in-law cry to each other about their lives.

"These men have to die before we can ever find happiness," Jean told her sister.

Joe was convinced she had a lover and wanted him out of the way. "I have tapes showing that my wife wanted me dead," he told the judge.

Luckily for Jean, the judge refused to listen and declared them inadmissible, but it tainted her grounds for claiming abandonment. She won her house, but had to give up alimony. Joe was bitter that he lost the house and saw himself as the victim once more.

Lost Treasures

Time gives no forewarning
As youth will have its way
Not caring for each morning
Or every precious day

The Lord gives us the freedom
To choose what we will do
If we just listen to his voice
Our soul he will renew

Give no care to things
You gain upon this earth.
Treasures will be left behind
To what you had at birth

— Gemini Joe

Joe became the villain in his children's eyes. He left his wife emotionally drained, questioning her past, uncertain about her future, and with no way to support herself. She put the house up for sale and planned to move to a small apartment.

Anna and her family left Texas and moved to Atlanta. Her brother Joey soon followed, buying a house on the other side of town.

"Come and stay with me," Anna offered her mother. "Once you sell the house, you'll have plenty of money to buy a house here."

Jean sent Linda ahead while she packed and put her furniture in storage. She agreed to take a chance on Georgia, leaving Dana behind with a toddler.

Jean stayed with Anna until she could get on her feet, trying to adjust to the fact that her life was changed forever. She was not happy and found it hard to move on, until Lucia called.

"Come to Florida, Jean. They're building townhouses two blocks away from me. I know you could be happy here."

Jean hadn't considered following her sister. Lucia moved to Florida to be close to her daughter so Jean thought it only natural to move close to hers.

"I'm free," Jean thought to herself. "Joe can't stop me from being with my sister." She pushed aside her fears and jumped in with both feet.

"Lucia! Put a deposit down on that townhouse for me! I'm coming to Florida!"

Anna was sad to see her mother go, but knew that she would be happier in the sun.

* * * * * *

Joe left behind a thirty-three year marriage to start a relationship with Ann and moved into the house she shared with her disabled son. She seemed to be a perfect match: a real go-getter who enjoyed the nightlife. Ann took the reins, and they became the "it" couple, dancing and laughing as they frequented local bars. He settled into the relationship with no excuse to be depressed. But he soon realized his relationship with Ann wasn't as perfect as he thought.

"Joe, you need to wipe down the tiles after you take a shower. And why is the soap wet? You need to put it on the rack after you use it," Ann complained.

"What? You have to be kidding," he stared in disbelief. Passive aggression, Joe's specialty, kept him from arguing. He made a mental note to keep his distance. Ann imagined a life together, but the pressure of commitment was too much for Joe. He resented being told what to do, and was not accustomed to her constant scrutiny. His inner demons began to peek out. Distance grew with every word they exchanged and Ann soon noticed that Joe was a needy man. Although Ann was the nurturing type, she sensed that she could not fix him.

Maybe he is not the one, she thought. She began to loosen her grip and allowed things to take their course.

After only three months, Joe found himself another place to live in Wantagh. Ann did not fight him when he announced that he was moving out. In fact, she was relieved. "We can still be friends," she promised. Even though Joe broke off the relationship, he felt like he had been kicked again. Ann watched him out the living room window as he left for good. Before he opened the door to his car, she saw him bending down over the garden hose. She wondered what he was doing, then saw him unscrew the nozzle and put it in his pocket. She knocked on the window to get his attention, but he jumped in his car and took off, leaving Ann with her mouth open in disbelief.

A Special Friend

I thank God for knowing a lady as thee,
Quiet ways and secrets, only I could see.
Your many hurts are hidden behind your smile,
But I know that it's your unique style.

When we first met, your qualities
came to view, your many thoughts
of things for us to do.
A friend forever you will always be to me,
For to me you are as solid as an old oak tree.

Though in this world we may never meet again,
To me you will always be my special friend.

— Gemini Joe

Joe wallowed in his loneliness, especially at night. He woke up every two hours, alone. Sometimes he could fall back asleep, but most nights he cried like a baby. He imagined his ex-wife surrounded by her family.

They must be blaming me for everything, he thought, feeling a familiar sense of persecution. It did not matter if it was day or night. The silence that surrounded him became a nightmare that was not restricted to the dark.

Maybe I'll get a dog, he thought.

He drove to the local animal shelter. "I'd like to adopt a puppy," he told the clerk.

"We don't have any puppies," she said, disinterested.

"I want a small dog," Joe insisted. "Can I look?"

"Yeah," she said, annoyed as she fumbled for the keys to the back and strained to raise her large body from the chair.

Joe looked into each cage. Most of the dogs were mutts and too large to keep in his small, rented room. He was about to leave when he noticed a small white dog curled up in a tiny cage. It had its back turned, so he could not see its face.

"What kind of dog is that?" Joe asked.

"That's a Yorkshire terrier, but she is kind of old." The attendant tried to discourage him from taking any further interest.

"Can I see her?" Joe insisted.

As soon as the cage was open, the little white dog jumped up and came to life. Joe looked into her old eyes and instantly fell in love. "That's my dog," he told the clerk. "I want her!"

Joe drove all the way home with the dog on his lap. She jumped up to lick his face. Basking in her unconditional love, he tried to think of a name. He thought about the most beautiful woman he knew of, Brigitte Bardot. "Brigitte, I will call you Brigitte."

* * * * * *

Joe missed his children. "Everyone left," he complained.

Anna and Joey lived in Georgia. His youngest daughter, Linda, lived in Florida with her mother, and he wasn't sure if he would ever see her again. Only Dana remained on Long Island, but she lived out east and the drive was long. Busy with her own family, she had little time or tolerance for her father. Joe was alone with his dog. Back at the bar, he cried about his life once again.

Regrets and Tears

What kind of fools us mortals be
To be given eyes but do not see

To know that time is surely spent
Then always wonder where it went.

We spend our life in hopes and fears
Then look back with regret and tears.

So take today for what it's worth
For tomorrow is someone else's birth.

— Gemini Joe

One October day, the phone rang in Joe's apartment. "Hi, Dad, how are you?"

"Linda, I'm so happy to hear from you, baby. I miss you so much!"

"I hate it here in Florida. It's too hot and I don't know anyone."

"Well, what do you expect? It's not New York. There's no place like New York."

"I want to come back home and live with you," she cried.

Joe became silent as he realized the consequences of her words. "Oh, baby, I only have a one bedroom apartment."

"I'll sleep on the couch. Please, Daddy, I miss you."

"Does your mother know?"

"She knows I'm not happy. Besides, I'm sixteen. I can decide for myself."

"Well, I guess I could give you my room and…"

Before he could finish his thought, Linda added, "Have you seen my boyfriend around? Tell him I'm coming back, if you see him."

Joe stared at the receiver for a long time before hanging up the phone. He didn't know if he should be happy or scared. On one hand, he won. His daughter wanted to live with him, not her mother. On the other hand, could he handle a teenager living in his small apartment? It was going to be a long, cold winter.

Within two weeks, Linda had a plane ticket back to New York. Jean begged her daughter to stay in Florida, but she could not handle Linda's anger. She was mad at her mother for moving off of Long Island, and felt out of place in Florida. She missed her friends and she also missed her sister Dana.

The minute Joe picked his daughter up from the airport, he began to regret his decision to let her live with him. But he smiled and cooed over his daughter in spite of his reservations. He hadn't seen her since she left in the spring. He didn't want her to regret choosing him over her mother.

"Dad, I need a car," Linda told him while walking to baggage claim to pick up her suitcases.

"Okay, baby. We'll look for a small car, but it will have to be used. I can't afford a new one."

"Great, Dad. Oh, and I also need to go to an eye doctor. I am tired of my glasses and I really would love to have contact lenses—green ones."

"Sure, honey, okay."

"I'm so happy to be home, Daddy! Thank you for letting me stay in your apartment. I promise not to get in the way, and I will clean and cook for you."

As they left the airport, a cold autumn breeze blew. Linda shivered.

"Where's your coat?" Joe asked his daughter.

"I guess I forgot to bring it," Linda smiled. "We may have to add that to the list, and boots too!"

Linda stood in the living room scanning the apartment. She didn't realize how small it would be.

"Where am I going to sleep," she asked her father.

"You can take my room if you like. I can sleep on the couch. It has a pullout bed." Joe hoped she would volunteer to sleep on the couch. He didn't want to give up his room.

But Linda rushed past him to put her luggage in the room. "Thanks, Dad."

"It's no problem, honey. I have to go out for a while. Are you going to be all right here alone?"

"Of course! As long as there is a phone and a television."

"Okay, then, I'll see you later."

Joe headed to the bar. He walked out to his car, unable to stop the jumble in his mind, lamenting his decision about Linda. She was already asleep when he returned and he could not get in the room to retrieve his pillow or a blanket. He stretched out on the couch, his feet hanging off the end, and passed out.

It only took a month before Joe began losing his temper. "Can't you pick up after yourself? And must you use every glass and towel in the place?" Joe asked in frustration. He was in over his head. He couldn't get his daughter to do anything. She refused to go to school and slept half the day away on his couch. He avoided the apartment when she was home, doing side jobs in the day and sitting at the bar every night.

Linda should be at school, Joe thought as he sprinted up the stairs two at a time on his lunch break. His lighthearted humor turned sour when he opened the door. They were on his couch, naked! His daughter and some strange guy!

"Get out of my house!" he yelled as the boy jumped up and hurried to pull his pants on. The boy grabbed his shirt and left his shoes behind, not turning to look back as he flew out the front door.

"Dad, what are you doing home from work so early?" Linda demanded, clutching the blanket around her chest. Joe shook his head with disappointment. He regretted allowing his daughter to move in with him and tried to figure out how to get her back to Florida. A few days later, he came up with a plan.

"I'm bringing Linda to Florida," Joe told his ex-wife. "We need to talk about getting back together, for her sake."

Linda was excited. She wanted to see her parents together and didn't mind giving the Sunshine State another chance if it meant they could be a family again. Joe felt guilty as they packed the last box and loaded it into the truck. He had no intention of living in Florida. His sister-in-law lived two blocks away from Jean's new townhouse. He had spent years trying to get away from Lucia.

"I knew she would follow her sister," he told his bar buddies. "I told you she couldn't function without her. My whole life I had to put up with that shit. She would have let her sleep with us if there had been room in the bed. That's how obsessed she is."

* * * * * *

The minute they crossed the Florida state line, Joe felt his lungs contract. Oppressive heat made it hard to breath. Like a hot iron, it scorched his throat and the sun's ray burnt his skin. By the time they reached their destination, Joe realized why his daughter had wanted to leave. Everything was different—even the food.

"They don't know how to make pizza here," he complained. "And look at that bread. It's like a wet sponge. Where are all the bakeries? Where's the pork store? There's nothing Italian about this place."

"Its paradise," Jean told him. "The skies are always blue and if it rains, it stops within an hour or two. You'll get used to it."

The Florida sun beat down on him and the humidity made him lose his breath. Forced to stay inside during the heat of the day, he sat on the couch and looked at his ex-wife.

"Let's go make some sauce like we used to," he said.

"I don't cook anymore!"

"Well, then, let's go upstairs and fool around," he smiled his sinister smile.

"What's in it for me?" Jean replied, refusing to jump at his every demand.

Joe knew he no longer had power. Once he was sure his daughter would stay in Florida, he planned his route back to New York. He disappeared one day, leaving behind a note for Jean and Linda. "I am going back to New York. I'm very sorry, but I can't live here in Florida. Please forgive me."

"Good riddance!" Jean thought. It was so much easier to say goodbye the second time.

* * * * * *

In New York, Joe stayed with friends while he looked for another apartment. He began to visit Dana more often. After crying that he did not have long to live, he weaseled his way into her house. "The doctor says I have throat cancer," he cried. "I have no one."

In a moment of weakness, Dana allowed him to move into her basement. Joe settled into the security of her family, enjoying hot home-cooked meals as he came and went to the bar. Joe started to treat his daughter more like his wife, complaining and criticizing everything she cooked. "Tell your kids to calm down," he insisted. "They're wild!"

He spent more time at the bar, using the children as an excuse. They heard him stumbling into the house all hours of the night.

"Grandpa's drunk again," the awakened children announced.

"Get out of here, you brats," he slurred, heading toward his dungeon.

Bump, bump, bump, bump! Dana heard Joe tumble down the stairs after a long night of drinking. She rolled over and went back to sleep. She could not hide his alcoholism from the children. Dana made up her mind. He had to go! The next morning, she waited for him to come upstairs for a cup of coffee.

"Dad, we need to talk," Dana said.

Joe sat at the table with his head in his hands. "Yeah, okay, but talk low, I have a headache."

"Tim thinks you should find another place to live," she said, blaming her husband. "You come in late every night and wake us up. It's just not working out, and we think you would be better off in your own place."

"Geez, I've only been here two months," Joe mumbled. After his coffee, he shook his head in disgust and drove off.

Joe was homeless once more. He retreated to his favorite bar for a quick scotch on the rocks, a tear or two, and a visit with the cute girl serving it. The waitress, Karen, was ten years younger than Joe. She was petite with blonde hair and blue eyes, but Joe decided that her hair color must have come from a bottle. She had a small frame and a bulbous bottom, but for the most part seemed to keep herself in good shape. He was instantly attracted to her and took every opportunity to flirt by making her laugh at his silly jokes. It didn't hurt that she owned her own home and lived alone. Like most people who first encountered Gemini Joe, Karen loved to talk with Joe. She enjoyed his charisma and thought he was a light-hearted soul. He was a good dancer and after a few drinks, he entertained the patrons with his talent. It wasn't long before Joe started dating Karen and spending time at her place. Things were going great!

Share a Log

Meet me at the lakeside
And sit with me on a log
Share with me the pleasures
As night winds blow away the fog

Watch as the sun rises high and bright
How the rays cut through the night
Born again in a new days beginning
The promise of a chance for winning

— Gemini Joe

Karen's twenty-four-year-old daughter, Becky, visited quite often, too often as far as Joe was concerned. She wasn't as pretty as her mother. Her long brown hair was unruly and in her face, hiding a bad case of acne. She relied on her mother and did not let one day go by without visiting or calling on the phone. Joe didn't like to share and made no effort to hide it. Mother and daughter felt Joe's jealousy. Karen made excuses for him, but her daughter was not as forgiving.

"I don't like him. He's not as good as he seems," Becky warned her mother. "I think you should get rid of him."

"I think I love him."

"He has nothing to offer. You don't need another bum in your life."

Becky was right, and it wasn't long before her mother faced the facts. She could not soothe Joe's jealous nature and she was tired of fighting. "I don't think it's working between us," she told him.

Joe promised to try harder. He didn't want to lose this woman. He tried to control his needs and jealousy, but it was no use. Maybe it was insecurity or the fear of losing something he loved, but the green-eyed monster always prevailed. He had been jealous of the relationship Jean had with her mother. When her mother died, he fixated on Jean's father. When he was gone, it was her sister and his children. Now he felt threatened by the relationship Karen had with her daughter. The realization of his loss came too late. He loved Karen and clung to her for dear life, but Karen escaped, leaving him heartbroken and alone.

Forgotten Love

Put it away they say of love
That lasted oh so long

Put it away like yesterday's glove
Or an old forgotten song

And so I have...I've put it away
Its ghost rises now and then

Reminding me of joyful days
That now are long forgotten

— Gemini Joe

Chapter Eighteen

Joe bought a trailer in Amityville, a few towns away from where he raised his family. Self-pity, an emotion familiar to Joe, presided as he sulked about losing Karen. She was his last hope of finding happiness. He cringed at the prospect of being alone again. He had no one to take care of him, to cook, to clean, to cut his toenails. He lost everything: his career, his home, his wife, and his sobriety. Dana wanted nothing to do with him, although she tried when everyone else moved out of New York, thinking he was the only family she had nearby. But he brought back too many bad memories and inflicted his deep-seated disrespect for women on her. Joe was a man, and he learned from his father that women only had one purpose. Although he loved his mother intensely, he didn't respect her for being a doormat. He resented her tolerance of his father and how she waited on his every need. If only she put her foot down, Joe often thought.

His trailer had a shed where he set up a small shop, perfect for building the projects that crowded his head. Through the smoke that filled this small space, he focused on creating birdhouses and birdfeeders with wood, glue, and paint. Fear of dying kept him working and looking over his shoulder. He felt that God was ready to take him away. Pretending to be very busy, he hoped God would let him stay and come back for him later.

Feeling creative, Joe began building lawn-sized lighthouses. He entered them in shows, winning prizes and admiration from everyone around him. Neighbors came by to say hello and check out his latest creations.

One day he sat in his recliner, enjoying the History Channel. Joe's eyes began to feel heavy as he floated into slumber. He was startled back into consciousness by the old-fashioned rotary phone on his table.

"Hello," he said in a sleepy voice.

"Your brother's dead!" a woman's familiar voice yelled into the receiver, before slamming the phone to hang up.

What? My mother's dead? No, she's been dead a long time, he thought, trying to regain his senses. She said that my brother is dead. But Dom died over a year ago. He only had one more brother, Franc. Then it hit him. The voice on the other end of the phone was the same shrill voice that told him his mother died. Mary had called to announce Franc's death. "What a cruel family I have," Joe said, shedding a tear for his brother.

At sixty-four years old, Joe was the only remaining Fuccino, besides his son. He had always thought he was indestructible. "I better go for a check-up," Joe decided. His mother died of cancer and both of his brothers too. He wasn't about to leave it to chance.

Joe filled out the medical questionnaire before he was taken to the examination room. He flirted with the nurse, forgetting his age and his reason for being there.

The doctor looked over Joe's chart, ignoring him as he sat on the end of the exam table. "Do you want to die, Joe?" his doctor asked him. "If you don't quit smoking, you won't live past six months."

Fear shook Joe as he became aware of his own mortality. He complained about his life, but he was not ready to give it up. Determined to stick around, he stopped smoking. As a boy, he smoked his first cigarettes by pretending to inhale, drawing the smoke into his mouth and stopping it before it went down his throat, and he quit the same way. Lighting one cigarette after another, he held it between his fingers and practiced smoking without inhaling. No longer dependent on cigarettes, Joe enjoyed his new lease on life.

* * * * * *

Joe spent time admiring the boats that dotted the Long Island Sound. He always wanted his own boat, but he could never afford one. As the weather began to cool off, boats came out of the water and settled on dry land for the winter. Their owners had had their fill of the sea. Some were tired of the maintenance and ready to escape the expense of docking. It was the best time to buy one, but Joe found the perfect boat in the boatyard dumpster. It was weathered and old with a broken motor, but that didn't bother him. He saw it as a challenge and an opportunity to create something from nothing. He stopped going to the bar. Scotch couldn't hold him while he rebuilt the boat and tinkered with the motor.

My Shadow is Cast

I am who I am and I know what I see
Until that day when I cease to be

My shadow I cast, upon this earth.
Until the final day, I recall my birth

Life is pleasant if you make it so
Life is over before you know

Little time for tears and stress
The time is now for happiness

— Gemini Joe

It was a hard winter, and he did not move as fast as he used to. Both he and his little dog felt the bite of the cold that made their joints ache. But, by spring, he basked in the sunshine on his new boat, and the pride he felt for accomplishing his task. Most people name boats after women, but "Gemini Joe," the bar name he embraced, seemed like the perfect name.

He spent many hours on the water, fishing and drinking O'Doul's. His bronzed body glistened in the sun and a white captain's hat shaded his eyes. Wisps of grey hair peeked out from his hat, but he was still a handsome man, especially when he smiled. Sometimes he just sat on the boat as it floated on the sea, pondering his life. The beauty of the ocean cleansed his soul while the gentle rocking of the boat soothed his uneasy spirit. The sea encouraged his artistic side, which he nurtured by painting and writing poetry. Large canvases sat in his trailer as he painted two or three oil paintings at one time. Art brought out his softer side and he began to let go of the bitterness he felt toward those around him. He was ready to reach out to his children, sending poetry and pictures of his lighthouses. One by one, they went to visit him in his new world. He looked different and sounded different to them. "Maybe he changed," they thought.

Anna decided to ask him if he would write down his childhood memories. Joe gave it his best shot, but could not get past four pages. The few pages that he did send made Anna realize there was a treasure trove of stories to be told. She coached him by phone, but it was too difficult for him.

"Baby, I can't write," he told her. "I'm not good at it and you won't be able to read my scribble."

Discouraged, Anna put the pages in a safe place and tried to forget about it. She found herself calling him on the phone to pick his brain, but it was hard to hear his voice and she felt like she was betraying her mother. But Anna refused to give up. She was determined to retrieve what was rightfully hers. Joe was never her daddy, but he was her father and she wanted to know what happened to him in his life to make him bitter and cynical.

Anna sent him a tape recorder and five tapes, along with five self-addressed envelopes. He was very excited about the project and eager to try it.

"This is very smart of you to think of a tape recorder. You must get that from me," he boasted.

At first he had trouble operating the piece of technology, so Anna called to instruct him how to use it and did not let up until he felt comfortable.

"This is great," he said. "I'm starting to get the hang of it and I'm having fun. I get tired and have to stop, but then I keep coming back to it." Joe was happy to make the tapes about his memories and was thrilled that his daughter showed interest in him.

After receiving the first envelope, Anna left it in her drawer for three days until she was ready to open it. She needed time. When she was feeling strong enough to listen to his voice, she popped the cassette into the player and braced herself. He sounded nervous as he said, "Hi, Anna, this is your Dad. I don't know if I can work this machine, but I will do my best." After starting and stopping the tape, he finally became comfortable and started telling the tale of his childhood.

Anna was surprised by the happiness she heard in his voice as he told her about memories long forgotten. After that, she anxiously waited for the mail. She was collecting the missing pieces of his life and, although it did not change the events of her childhood, she had an understanding of the man behind the alcoholic.

Tearfully he said, "I want to thank you! Making these tapes was a very hard thing to do, but it has shown me that my life was not as bad as I imagined. I have very good memories about my family, and these tapes allowed me to revisit the good times in my life. It brought back my mother's face and many happy times that I have buried over the years."

Joe told his daughter many things about his youth. Some of them were endearing and some revealed things that shaped his personality. "I'm so sorry," he insisted. "I didn't want things to turn out this way."

Anna wanted to believe him. Maybe he realized the damage he caused his family. But it didn't take long for her to realize he was up to his old tricks, seeking pity while he felt sorry for himself. "Everyone has left now and the family has split. I am so alone," he whined. "I wish things were different. I wish my children would all come back to New York. I had to leave your mother. She never loved me and I couldn't live like that. She had a lover, you know."

Anna began to get that old, familiar feeling, deep inside. She quickly changed the subject back to his poetry. "Dad, I had no idea that you wrote poetry. How long have you been writing?"

"I've been writing all my life. You just never had an interest."

"I never knew. I'd like to read more," she coached.

"I'm so lonely, baby. It's nice that you care about me."

The price for his art was high. Anna had to endure long phone conversations that turned from pleasant to pathetic, diverting his constant complaining about how her mother ruined his life.

"I could have done so much with my life. Your mother held me back. She took my children away," he cried. "I know you don't want to hear about it."

Anna made no effort to console him. "I already know these things, Dad."

"Let me tell you something!" He recited his old mantra. "Some day you're going to know the truth."

"She's my mother. I don't know what you want me to say."

"Eh! You don't care! I'm so depressed." He waved his hand to dismiss her as the familiar words came from his mouth.

Anna bit her tongue. She could never figure out if he was disgusted with her or with the fact that she did not sympathize with his pain. Something inside told her it was the latter, but the effect was still the same. He always managed to make her feel like something was wrong with her.

Thankfully, she lived too far away to deal with his life-sucking emotions. She kept the relationship based on phone calls and hung up when her ears hurt. "Sorry, Dad, but I have to go now. I'll talk to you again really soon."

* * * * * *

While in New York to attend a funeral, Joey and his wife, Kendal, paid his father a visit.

"I'm so lonely," Joe cried.

"Dad, there's no reason to feel lonely. Stop whining! Get out and do something! Make some friends!"

"But I don't feel good."

His daughter-in-law did not know him well. Her heart was breaking for the old man, sitting in his chair as they said goodbye to each other.

"I think you should let him come and live with us," she tried to convince her husband.

"You don't know him. He's not easy to live with."

"I don't care. He is your father and you should help him."

"I'll think about it," he promised, hoping she would forget.

The hot Georgia sun beat down on the deck as Anna and Joey watched their kids swim in the pool. They lived an hour apart, but only got together on occasion. They made it a point to meet for lunch once a month.

"I talked to Dad the other day. He's not doing too well," he informed his sister.

"You know he's a crier," Anna reminded him.

"Yeah, but I feel bad for him. Kendal and I have been thinking about moving him down here. We have plenty of room and he could rent my basement."

"What? Do you know what you're saying?" Anna was shocked. "Don't do it. You will be sorry."

"Kendal thinks it is wrong to leave him there alone. After all, he is our father. As his only son, I feel like I need to help him."

"He has problems and he is going to pull you and your family into dysfunction."

"Kendal thinks it would be good for the kids to have him around."

"What? Dad and Kendal's kids? He never even liked his own. What makes you think he will be better with hers?"

But no words could dissuade him. He had his mind made up.

"You're going to be sorry," Anna warned him. But she was nervous. If her father lived so close, she would have no excuse not to see him more often. It was much more comfortable to maintain a long-distance relationship.

Anna hoped that her brother would forget about it, but before the summer was over, he was on his way back from New York, their father in the front seat with his dog, Brigitte, and all his belongings in a trailer behind them.

Joe had cried wolf, not thinking someone would actually try to save him. When his son tossed him the life preserver, he had no choice. Things happened fast, and Joe went with the flow, thinking maybe he would find love and a new family. Georgia seemed like another world. Well, maybe it will be nice, Joe thought. I'll give it a chance.

Before he left New York, he said goodbye to his friends.

Scooter's Den

I give a toast to Scooter's, and all my newfound pals
A place with friendly faces, and many pretty gals

An oasis in the desert, where there is a good chance
That any given moment, you can find romance

With regrets, I must leave the Den
But I hope to come this way again

Now I leave with a tear in my eye
Farewell as I bid all a heartfelt goodbye

— Gemini Joe

* * * * * *

Leaving all his worldy possessions to his son upon his death, he would live rent-free for the rest of his life. There would be no inheritance when he died, nothing to divide between his three daughters. "There will be nothing to fight about," he thought to himself, thinking about his own father.

He wasn't prepared for what he found. Water puddles sat in front of the back door, the smell of mildew filling the room. Joe's heart sank as he realized breathing was going to be a problem. A vision of his father-in-law flashed through his mind. I wonder if this is how he felt, when I moved him into the basement, Joe asked himself. He spent his money fixing up an apartment in the basement

"Let's go to the hardware store and buy supplies," Joe said to his son, trying to be cheerful. Impatient, he pushed his son to work on the apartment. Together they put in the plumbing, electricity, and sheetrock. They worked every night and every weekend.

At least it's keeping them busy, Anna thought. She only had to endure a couple of dinners now and then.

When Joe moved in, Kendal thought she was getting a new dad and a grandpa for her two children from a previous marriage. "Remember, Dad, they need to listen to you. Feel free to yell at them if they do something wrong." But it did not take long before friction between her children and Joe threatened the family unity.

"I hate him," Kendal's son announced in his mother's car on the way to school. "He yells all the time and he is mean."

"Your son is unruly and he does not pick up after himself," Joe accused. "He is wild and runs around the house and teases my dog."

"He feeds his dog on the couch," Kendal's son tattled.

Joey found himself playing mediator every night. Even though he was tired from working all day, he quickly put his dinner dish in the sink and turned to his father. "Let's get to work on that apartment." He could not build it fast enough.

"Why didn't you build the apartment before you moved Dad down here?" Anna asked her brother.

"He is on my back all the time. Kendal and I are constantly fighting because he keeps yelling at her kids. I don't know what to do."

When Kendal packed up and left with her kids, only father and son remained.

Joey was distraught. He was mad at his wife for leaving, but he felt an obligation to his father. After all, he talked him into leaving New York, but now he wished that he would have left his father in his trailer.

"She was no good anyway!" Joe told his son.

At his father's harsh words, Joey realized his mistake. He wanted his wife back, but she refused to come home as long as her father-in-law was living in the house. It didn't take long before Joe sucked the energy out of his only son, demanding total attention and causing hard feelings when he didn't get it. Avoidance seemed the only solution, and he began to stay over at Kendal's apartment more often. He stopped working on the basement apartment, which annoyed Joe, who had spent most of his life savings on the material. Everyday, Joe waited for his son to come home. Disagreements turned into fights and fights caused Joey to walk out of the house, leaving his father to sit and feel sorry for himself.

"If I'm late coming home from work, he gives me the third degree. He keeps pressuring me to work on the apartment, but I don't feel like it. I can't take it anymore," he complained to Anna.

The only walls going up were between Joe and his son. Neither of them knew how to get out of the living situation. Joe didn't want to admit he made a mistake and his son didn't want to tell him to leave. Joe sold his trailer and his boat in New York. Now he had no home.

"I don't feel good," Joe announced after dinner.

"You're a grown man. Go to the doctor!"

"Could you take off from work tomorrow and take me?"

"No, I have to go in to work tomorrow. Make an appointment for next week."

Joe knew his son was putting him off, but he could not wait. He woke up the next morning and went to the doctor. Something was wrong, he was sure.

"He'll feel bad when he realizes that I am really sick," Joe thought. He didn't really think it was serious, but thought he could get pity. The doctors' results threw him off balance and he rushed home to wait for his son. He sat by the window, straining to see each car come down the street. Still in shock from the news, Joe held back the tears, refusing to waste them until his son came home. Finally, the truck pulled up the driveway. The curtain moved as he jumped into his position on the couch.

"I'm sick, Joey. I'm very sick."

"What's wrong, Dad?"

"The doctor says I have prostate cancer." Tears began to flow as he choked on the words. "I'm going to die."

"You're not going to die. They just need to give you chemotherapy or radiation."

"I need to go home. I don't trust these doctors. I need to go back to New York."

"Are you sure?"

"Yes, I want to go home."

Empathy was now easier to give, since Joey felt relief was on the way.

"If you really want to go, I'll put in for some vacation time and take you back."

"Yes, that's what I want."

They sat down for dinner, neither one finding more words than necessary. Joe was anxious to go home, and Joey was anxious to get him there. It happened so fast that Anna only spent one more afternoon with him. She could see the resentment peeking out from his eyes when he mentioned his son.

"He made me spend all my money on building supplies. I don't care. I just have to get away from him," Joe told Anna. His plan backfired and he only had enough money left to get back to New York.

******

Joe arrived back in New York on a hot summer day. He arranged to stay with a friend who owned a bar with an apartment above. The apartment was always empty because the tenants couldn't sleep through the loud music that blasted from downstairs. He settled in with his dog until he could find a permanent place to live. His next stop was the trailer park where he lived before. The landlord was happy to see him, but didn't have a trailer in his price range. Most of his money was gone, and all he had left was three thousand dollars and his monthly pension. As he was leaving, his friend remembered an old trailer that needed work.

"Joe, I may have something, but it's in bad shape."

They walked across the trailer park to an old, rotting structure. It was a mess, with leaks in the roof and bad plumbing. Paint was peeling off the walls and the florescent lights flickered on and off in the kitchen, giving it an eerie glow. Joe looked around sadly as he noticed the buckling floor panels in the living room and the large window that faced the adjoining trailer, only two feet away.

"I'll take it," he said, trying to hide his disappointment. He bought the broken-down home for two thousand dollars and, considering it a challenge, felt happy to be back in New York. The first night he spent in the trailer, it rained. He tossed and turned as he listened to the drip, drip, drip in the bucket, making mental notes on what needed fixing first. Even his dog, Brigitte, was having nightmares. He held her close and let his tears flow.

Lonely Heart

Go to sleep my lonely heart
Let memories rest or do depart
No greater pain can life endure
It prays on all, the rich and poor.

Lonely can be dark and empty
Each day passes like a century
Somewhere there is peace and joy
A treasure searched by girl and boy

— Gemini Joe

It took most of his energy and time to make the place livable, but he found the strength through anger.

"When are you going to send me the money from the building supplies?" he asked his son. "You promised that you would reimburse me for the material I bought to finish your basement."

"I can only send you a little at a time. You'll get your money," Joey promised. "My wife has come back home with the kids and she isn't working right now."

Bitterness spread through Joe like a wildfire. He couldn't be happy for his son because "the bitch won." She drove a wedge between them, father and son. He was forced out of the house and now they were once again a happy family, of which he couldn't be a part.

The high humidity on Long Island meant no easy breathing for Joe. He bought an air conditioner and locked himself into the trailer.

"Joe, don't call it a 'trailer,' this is a 'mobile home,'" his neighbors insisted. Joe did not care what it was called. He felt safe and secure with Brigitte. She, too, was older and having a little trouble. She had arthritis in her left leg and limped when she tried to walk. She spent the day sleeping on her little bed while Joe sat in his chair.

"We're getting old together," he told the little dog, who raised her head and wagged her tail when she heard his voice. Joe preferred his dog to people, and felt anger toward everyone else.

While bitterness took over his soul, cancer took over his body. It began with prostate cancer. Months of chemotherapy and radiation stopped it in its tracks, but as soon as he thought he was safe, he discovered that he had bladder cancer. Thoughts of his mother's struggle reinforced his fear. He ran to doctors, crying and begging for them to save him. Then throat cancer robbed him of his voice. It was hard to know what was growing faster: the cancer or the hatred he felt for those around him. Crying to his neighbors had an effect at first. They felt bad for an old man whose family didn't seem to care about him.

"What is wrong with your children? Shame on them! They should be taking care of you." They offered to take him to his doctor's appointments and sit with him in his trailer for hours while he complained. Like a leech, he depleted their concern. Too soon they would make their escape and he would have to find another bleeding heart. He wanted very much to be the victim, twisting events in his mind. Eventually people discovered the truth. He was the one who divorced his wife and left his family.

As Joe was about to get into the shower, he heard the phone ringing. He shut off the water as he answered the phone. "Hello?"

"Hi, Uncle Joe?" It was a woman's voice.

"Who is this?"

"It's your niece! I have my mom here and she wants to talk to you. Here she is."

"Joe! Joe, it's Dolly, your sister. I've been trying to find you, and my daughter looked you up on her computer."

"Dolly, I'm so happy to hear your voice. Maybe you could come to visit."

"I can't, Joe. My knees gave out and I needed an operation. I am in wheelchair. I have diabetes and a bum heart. But I'll write to you and send you some pictures of my family."

"I'd like that very much. I can't believe our family was torn apart. Pop did not do right! He made us all fight."

"I love you Joey! You'll always be my baby brother. Take care of yourself."

"I love you too," Joe answered. "Goodbye for now." Joe hung up the receiver and did not feel so alone. Over the months, he corresponded with his sister, sharing memories and pictures. She was a lifeline to his past.

The next time his niece called, it was to inform him of her mother's death.

"She died in her sleep of heart failure. She died real peaceful, didn't feel a thing."

Joe was discouraged by the news of his sister's death, and began to accept his own fate. He convinced a friend to take him back to Brooklyn, back to the cemetery where his mother, father, two brothers, and sister were waiting. Joe outlived them all, but he felt no joy. Emphysema made life inconvenient as he attached himself to the oxygen hose that helped him breathe.

The next time Anna was in New York, she decided to pay him a visit. Sitting on the couch in his living room, she felt sick at the smell of mold and urine.

Joe made his way into the kitchen and stood in front of the sink. He braced himself as he attempted to convulse up phlegm, but his efforts were nonproductive. He took a deep breath and tried once more to dispel the obstruction in his throat. Nothing. The third time, he used his diaphragm and managed to spit into the sink. Anna recalled the many mornings that he coughed into the kitchen sink when she was growing up. The sound of his hacking every morning seemed to shake the house. It was gross then and it was gross now. She turned her head and pretended not to notice.

"Your mother ruined our lives," he said as he returned to his chair.

"I don't think she was totally to blame," Anna defended her.

"Let me tell you something," he snapped. "Your mother was cheating on me!"

"What?" Anna said, as she checked her surroundings. Joe had a way of always taking her back to Elm Street, sitting on the dining room chair.

"Why don't you open the window?" she coached, longing for fresh air.

Anna rose to get relief before he could answer. Her head

began to spin and she felt dizzy. She wasn't sure if it was the stuffiness or the words that came out of his mouth.

He rose from his chair and popped a meals-on-wheels meal into the microwave. Anna arranged for the benefit because he complained that no one would know if he died in his trailer. She figured he would have a meal and someone to check on him everyday.

At first, he balked. "I don't want that food. It's garbage." He would pick through it and stick some in the freezer, in case of an emergency. However, he eventually made friends with the deliveryman and started looking forward to the meal everyday.

"That's why I had to leave her," he continued. "She had a secret boyfriend. I heard her talking to him on the phone."

"Dad, I think you're mistaken." Anna tried to give him the benefit of the doubt and decided that he was delusional. Maybe his brain was swelling from all the radiation.

"I know you don't believe me! But your mother had a lover. Where do you think she went every night? She was meeting him."

"She went to bingo every night to be with her girlfriends. She didn't have a boyfriend." Anna was starting to get annoyed.

"She never loved me because she had someone else. I almost caught her, but she was too sneaky."

"I really don't want to hear anymore," she pleaded.

"You always take your mother's side. You just don't want to see the truth. You never did!"

There was no convincing him. Anna felt betrayed. She wanted the father who wrote poetry and painted pictures. She wanted the father who told her stories about Brooklyn, bringing her to the edge of long lost memories, not the vindictive, bitter man that sat in front of her. She wanted to walk away for good, but she was not finished getting her story. Letting him vent, she tried to relax and use his resentment as a vehicle into his soul. She knew he couldn't help himself. He was trying to justify his actions. He could not bear to be the bad guy. He wanted attention, he wanted pity, and he wanted love. Anna knew that was the reason behind his outrageous accusations, but it didn't make their meetings any easier. Even speaking on the phone was difficult. It hurt her ears when he veered off any subject and turned it toward his resentment.

"Do you know that your mother didn't care about her children? Your sister Dana almost drowned once because your mother wasn't watching her. I cried! I could not protect my baby!

Then there was the time when she laid Linda on the bed and walked away. The baby fell onto the floor and I was frantic. Your mother said it was not big deal. What mother does that?"

"It's okay, Dad!" Anna lied. "Put it behind you! There's no use in going back." She bit her tongue as she let him go on about her mother. She knew that he was trying to manipulate her. He mistakenly thought that she felt empathy for him because she continued to keep him in her life and called him every week. But Anna felt a surge of relief when she ended each call, sometimes throwing her phone aside in disgust.

* * * * * *

Joe sat alone in his trailer with his oxygen tank and television, surrounded by the pictures he painted and the artifacts he renovated. He missed his dog, Brigitte. He was always afraid that he would die before her, but he wasn't prepared for her to go first. It broke his heart when he drove her to the vet to be put to sleep, but she was in so much pain. He couldn't bear to hear her whimper when she tried to walk.

Not knowing if it was day or night, he drifted in and out of consciousness, his mind playing back the events of his life. Tears flowed in the darkness of night to wash away his anger. Acceptance came as a relief and he closed his eyes, waiting for death. He was too tired to fight.

The memory of his father loomed before him in the darkness, haunted by his father's cries of "mama, mama," that echoed through the halls of the hospital before he sucked in his last breath. Joe purposely waited until it was too late before entering his father's room. He stared down at the bully who tormented his family, now powerless and still, with his eyes protruding from his head. His lifeless body was still clenched, as if to prevent his soul from finding peace. "Mean bastard!" he said to the shell of the man he called his father.

The physical and emotional abuse he suffered in his childhood left him unable to grieve. He spent a lifetime trying not to be like his father. As he neared the end of his life, he found more in common with him than he wanted. He faced the same painful death. Fear kept him close to his nebulizer as he hung on to the poorest quality of life. Like a baby taking his first breath of life, he sucked in air with stubborn determination. He knew that his time was coming but refused the surgical airway his doctors offered, insisting on coughing up the poison on his own. Soon coughing would be futile and his lungs will fill with fluid or his heart will strain to its breaking point.

He once had a family, a home, and a promising career, but he drowned himself in alcohol to relieve the torment inside his head. Consumed by his quest for admiration, he lost everything he held dear. He loved his wife in the unhealthiest way — not satisfied unless he possessed her thoughts and soul. He didn't know how to love his children, twisting the roles of parent and child to suit his need for comfort. His demand for attention and love pushed everyone away until he was alone. Convinced that no one loved him, his worst fears came true in a self-fulfilling prophecy.

Joe spent 30 years trying to make his wife love him, only to push her away with his jealous nature and drunken rages. He remained embittered and spent most of his time bemoaning his fate. Joe whined about how he had wasted the best years of his life, how he worked everyday of his life to bring home a paycheck, how he was doomed to spend the end of his life alone. "If only my mother did not die...If only your mother loved me...If only, if only."

Childhood wounds inflicted a deep-seated self-pity that was hard to deny and he never ran out of new reasons to feel sorry for himself. Like a dog licking his wounds, Joe took comfort in his self-sorrow. Self-pity consumed the energy he could have used to turn his life around. Instead of dealing with his problems, he relished his misery, seeking empathy from those around him in a desperate cry for help. By taking solace at the bottom of a bottle, he created a vicious cycle of insecurity, anger, and tears.

Joe refused to see how he affected the people in his life and convinced himself that he was the victim. He was unaware of the damage he caused, but it was hard not to feel sorry for him in his self-created loneliness. He did not realize that feeling sorry for himself caused more damage to his life than the people he blamed. Anger and self-pity consumed him until all that was left was a pathetic man. His childlike ignorance made it hard for his children to hate him. He was just a man — a rotten husband, a terrible father, an abused brother, and the apple of his mother's eye.

Anna reflected on her own unhappiness. She could either do nothing, like her father, or take steps to change her life. The time spent listening to his story gave her the confidence to overcome her fear of change, and a strange peace settled in her heart. She knew what she had to do. Anna smiled as he wretched about his life…not because she was happy, but because it was the fire she needed to move away from the heat.

Janet Sierzant

Light of Life

Light of life grows ever dim
As many years pass by

A chance for love and peace so slim
So easy now to cry

God created man
In likeness of his own

In hope for love and peace on earth
But man can't stand alone

Sorrow comes much too quick
As Father Time leads on

Man will stand with weight of plow
In hope for sweeter song

Search for love and joy
The things that matter most

The search of every girl and boy
As Father Time keeps host

Quickly now, the end draws near
Man's body, tired and worn

To find the eyes bring quick a tear
And hope for love reborn

Light of life grows ever dim
Yet, man does his best to try

Chances seem so very slim
Still man searches till he dies

— Gemini Joe

Epilogue

His time is drawing near. Phone calls are shorter now as Joe struggles to find his voice. Systems are shutting down and he can no longer swallow his food.

"When was the last time you ate?" Anna asks.

"Yesterday I had a bite of oatmeal."

"Dad, you need to eat!"

"I can't eat. I feel full."

Stomach pains invade his sleep as he shivers in the dark. Anna tries to put herself in his place: in a dark room with no one to hear her cries. She feels a tinge of nausea and quickly distances herself from the feeling. "I need to find the strength to go back," she vows. Once again she pictures him sitting in his chair in his filthy trailer, alone, knowing there is no one. A chill runs up her spine and she feels a lump in her throat.

What could I do? I can't jump on a plane and go sit with him. He has been dying for so long. I would probably be wasting my time, only to get another call in a few months. I don't wish him pain. Maybe I should call again tonight, she thinks.

"Hi, Dad, how are you doing?"

"My friend is coming to pick me up in a few minutes. I'm going to bingo." The roller coaster continues to creep up slowly, and then wham! "I was told that I have lung cancer. I only have another year to live, but its okay. I'm not really living now. I can't hold on forever."

Joe's son jumps in his truck and drives sixteen hours to New York.

"I'm going to make sure Dad gets to see Linda before he dies. She hasn't seen Dad in over fifteen years and he is crying to see her."

Joe is so happy to see his youngest daughter. They spend three days talking and laughing until it is time for her to go home. They both say their tearful goodbyes.

"You probably won't see me again, baby," Joe tells Linda, self-pity always first and foremost in his mind.

Joey stays for a few more days, cooking and fixing things around the house. When he leaves, Joe sits in his chair staring at the television. He is alone once more. News that Jean suffered a stroke takes him by surprise.

"I wish her well," he says. But his empathy is short-lived when he discovers that his son, who is supposed to come back next month, decides to visit his mother instead.

"She needs me more than you do, Dad! I'll come back to New York in August."

"That bitch stole my thunder again," Joe fumes, jealous of the attention his ex-wife is receiving. When he hears that she fell in the hospital, he replies, "She probably did it on purpose so everyone would feel guilty for leaving her alone."

Joe is tired of thinking about it and decides to pack up his oxygen tank and drive to the supermarket for some ice cream. As he leaves the market, he backs out of the parking spot. Not paying attention, he hits the car next to him and drags the bumper off. For a second, he stops the car then steps on the gas. He looks around to see if there are any witnesses, but he is driving so fast, he can't be sure. By the time he arrives home, he is out of breath. Anxiety closes his throat and he panics. He reaches for the phone to dialed 911, causing his son to drive back to New York.

"He can't live alone anymore," he tells Anna. "I'm bringing him back to Georgia with me."

"Are you sure?" Anna asks, concerned for her brother.

"I have to! I can't let him die alone. I'll move him to a hospice down the road from my house."

Anna walks into his hospice room and stares at her father's weak, thin body, once strong and forceful. She can see the diaper he wears as the sheet falls from his fragile leg.

"Dad, are you awake?" Anna whispers.

Joe's eyes open wide. "Baby, when did you come to New York?"

"We're in Georgia, Dad. Don't you remember? Joey drove you down here so that you would not be alone."

"Oh, yeah. I want to go to his house."

"The nurses say that you have to stay in hospice, Dad. Just until they regulate your medicine," Anna lies. "Are you in pain?"

"No! I just can't breathe and I'm very tired."

"Do you need anything, Dad?"

"Yes, I need a nail file. Do you see this nail? It's too long."

"I have one in my car," Anna says. "I'll go get it."

On her way to retrieve the nail file, Anna debates whether she really wants to file his nails. She has never been a touchy person and does not relish the idea of getting too close to others, including members of her family.

"Which nail do you want filed?" she asks. Once she files the nail, she decides to file them all. It is the only intimacy she has had with her father since she was a baby.

After sitting with him for an hour, it is time to leave. "Dad, I have to go to Florida tomorrow to check on Mom, but I'll be back next month." Anna knows that he might not be there when she returns, but acts as if he will be waiting.

"Okay, baby, you have a safe trip and tell your mother that I wish her well."

Anna leaves the room, keeping her eyes straight ahead, but before she exits his room, her eyes turn toward him. He lay very still with his eyes closed. It is the last vision she has of her father. Before she arrives home, she can't remember if she told her father that she loves him. She picks up her phone.

"Joey, I need to talk to Dad."

"He's eating pizza right now. We'll call you when he is done."

Anna keeps the phone close by and answers it on the first ring.

"I'm going to put the phone up to Dad's ear," Joey says.

"Dad, Dad, I love you," Anna begins to cry. "I want you to know that and I don't remember if I told you."

"I love you too, baby! Joey brought me pizza and now I am going to have ice cream."

"That's great, Dad. I'm sorry that I have to leave tomorrow, but I just want you to know that I love you."

"I know! I love you too! Don't worry about me. Joey and his wife are taking good care of me."

"Okay, Dad. I'll talk to you while I'm on the road."

Two hours after crossing the Florida-Georgia line, Anna receives a phone call.

"Anna! Dad fell!"

"What? How did he fall? Did he hit his head? Is he all right?"

"No, no! He isn't good. He's just laying here, He's not talking. The nurses gave him something for pain."

"Call me later," Anna pleads, driving through a nasty rainstorm.

"This is it! They are starting the morphine." Anna could not understand her brother through his tears.

"Are you sure?"

"Yes, I'm staying here tonight. I can't leave him."

Anna holds tightly to the steering wheel while tears well up in her eyes.

"Please, God, take him quick. Don't let him suffer," she prays, recalling her father's fear of suffocating. At 2:30 A.M., she thinks he may be gone. At 6:30 A.M., she calls her father's room. A sleepy voice answers and she almost doesn't recognize her brother's voice.

"I've been here all night and didn't get much sleep. His arms are flailing and his eyes open when the nurses give him his medicine. He hasn't eaten anything in twenty-four hours. I want to keep him hydrated, but they say that I can't. It's hard to see him deteriorating in front of my eyes."

"I think you should get a music player and let him hear some music," Anna suggests. "He always loved Frank Sinatra and Dean Martin. It might sooth him. I don't want him to be scared."

"I called for the priest to give him his last rites. I have his hand and I am talking to him. He looks peaceful."

"I should have waited another day," Anna tells her brother.

"No. You take care of Mom. I have my wife and daughter by my side and they are helping me get through this. Call me every hour."

Anna's brother spends the next night at his father's bedside, sleeping for an hour at a time until morning. The nurses come in every four hours to administer more medicine. I wish this would end soon, but the nurse says that some people live up to thirty days without food or water, Joey thinks. He kisses his father's forehead until he tastes the morphine seeping through Joe's skin. Running into the bathroom he grabs a wash cloth and returns to scrub his father's face.

Suddenly, a gurgling sound alerts him. He rings for the nurse, not wanting to leave his father's side.

"Help him," he pleads.

"I'm afraid that this is the process," the nurse says sympathetically.

"Isn't there something you could do?"

"Well, maybe we could suction his lungs and make him more comfortable."

"Please, please do that for my father."

Joe's breathing is shallow, but he breathes a little easier after they clear his lungs.

"Tell him it's okay to leave. Tell him not to be scared. Tell him his mother is waiting for him on the other side," Anna begs.

"Dad, your job is done. You can put the hammer down."

Joe opens his eyes one last time and takes a deep breath before he leaves. His son opens the window so his spirit can soar.

Gemini Joe

The Twins

Joe as a child

Biker Joe

Joe with his new car

Joe on his boat

Janet Sierzant

Best Friends

Gemini Joe

GI Joe

Janet Sierzant

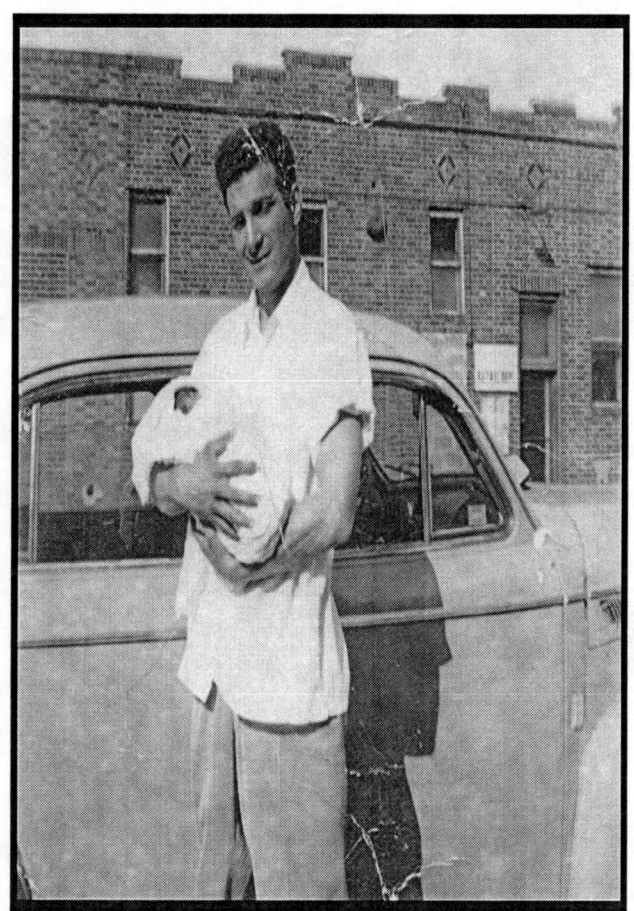

A New Dad

Pool Shark Joe

Janet Sierzant

Introducing Jean to the Family

Gemini Joe

Cowboy Joe

Janet Sierzant

One More for the Road

Gemini Joe

Afternoon break from work

Janet Sierzant

Life of the Party